Alfred's Kid's Guitar Course

Complete

Y0-AGU-304

The Easiest Guitar Method Ever!

Ron Manus • L.C. Harnsberger

This book is dedicated to Jennifer, Genevieve, Patrese, and Catherine Harnsberger, all of whom inspired many of the lyrics in this book.

Special thanks to Kate Westin, Bruce Goldes, Mark Burgess, Ted Engelbart, everyone at Alfred, and Daisy Rock Guitars.

Cover and interior illustrations by Jeff Shelly. Interior photos by Karen Miller.

Alfred Music Publishing Co., Inc.
16320 Roscoe Blvd., Suite 100
P.O. Box 10003
Van Nuys, CA 91410-0003
alfred.com

ISBN-10: 0-7390-4169-X (Book & CD)
ISBN-13: 978-0-7390-4169-7 (Book & CD)

ISBN-10: 0-7390-5888-6 (DVD)
ISBN-13: 978-0-7390-5888-6 (DVD)

Contents

Selecting Your Guitar

Guitars come in different types and sizes. It's important to choose a guitar that's just the right size for you, and not one that's too big.

TOO BIG!

Just right.

Guitars come in three basic sizes: 1/2 size, 3/4 size, and full size. You should look and feel comfortable holding your guitar, so it's a good idea to have your local music store's guitar specialist evaluate if your guitar is the right size.

If the 1/2 size guitar is still too big for you, a baritone ukulele can be used instead of a guitar to learn everything up to page 74 of this course.

Baritone uke   1/2 size   3/4 size   Full size

Steel Strings and Nylon Strings

Steel strings are found on both acoustic and electric guitars. They have a bright and brassy sound.

Nylon strings are usually found on classical and flamenco guitars. They have a mellow, delicate sound. Nylon strings are often easier for beginners to play because they are easier on the fingers than steel strings.

5

Acoustic Guitars and Electric Guitars

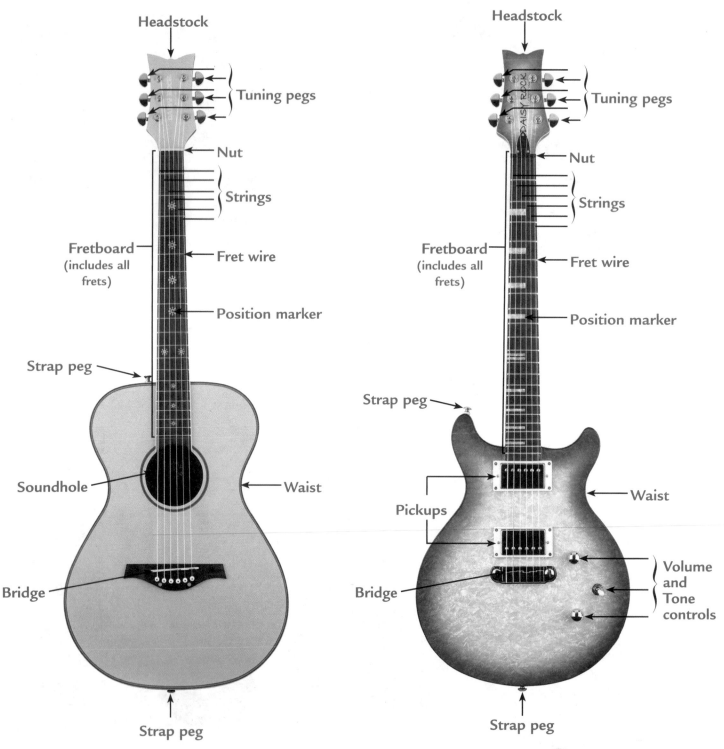

Headstock

Tuning pegs

Nut

Strings

Fretboard (includes all frets)

Fret wire

Position marker

Strap peg

Soundhole

Waist

Bridge

Strap peg

Headstock

Tuning pegs

Nut

Strings

Fretboard (includes all frets)

Fret wire

Position marker

Strap peg

Pickups

Waist

Bridge

Volume and Tone controls

Strap peg

Caring for Your Guitar

Get to know your guitar and treat it like a friend. When you carry it, think of it as part of your body so you don't accidentally bump it against walls or furniture, and be especially sure not to drop it! Every time you're done playing, carefully dust off your guitar with a soft cloth, and be sure to put it away in its case.

Tuning Your Guitar

First make sure your strings are wound properly around the tuning pegs. They should go from the inside to the outside, as in the picture. Some guitars have all six tuning pegs on the same side of the headstock, and in this case make sure all six strings are wound the same way, from inside out.

Turning a tuning peg clockwise makes the pitch lower. Turning a tuning peg counter-clockwise makes the pitch higher. Be sure not to tune the strings too high because they could break!

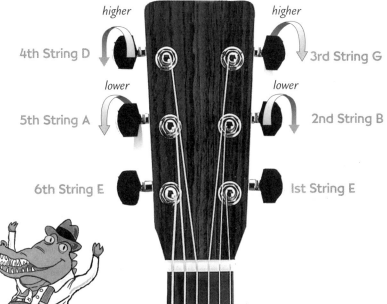

Important:

Always remember that the thinnest, highest-sounding string, the one closest to the floor, is the first string. The thickest, lowest-sounding string, the one closest to the ceiling, is the sixth string. When guitarists say "the highest string," they mean the highest-sounding string.

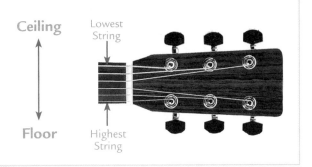

CD 1, CD 2
Tracks 1 & 2

Tuning with the CDs

Using Your CD Player
Put CD 1 or CD 2 in your CD player and play Tracks 1 and 2. Listen to the directions and match each of your guitar's strings to its pitch on the CD.

Using Your Computer
Put CD 1 or CD 2 in your computer's CD-ROM drive and click on "Tuning Your Guitar" in the table of contents. Follow the directions and listen carefully to get your guitar in tune.

Tuning without the CDs

Tuning the Guitar to Itself
When your sixth string is in tune, you can tune the rest of the strings just using the guitar alone. First, tune the sixth string to E on the piano, then follow the instructions to the right to get the guitar in tune.

Press 5th fret of 6th string to get pitch of 5th string (A).

Press 5th fret of 5th string to get pitch of 4th string (D).

Press 5th fret of 4th string to get pitch of 3rd string (G).

Press 4th fret of 3rd string to get pitch of 2nd string (B).

Press 5th fret of 2nd string to get pitch of 1st string (E).

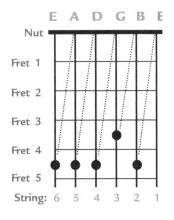

Pitch Pipes and Electronic Tuners
If you don't have a piano available, buying an electronic tuner or pitch pipe is recommended. The salesperson at your music store can show you how to use them.

How to Hold Your Guitar

Hold your guitar in the position that is most comfortable for you. Some positions are shown below.

Sitting

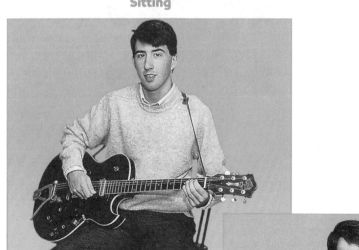

Sitting with legs crossed

Standing with strap

When you practice on your own or want to play just for fun, you might feel comfortable sitting cross-legged on the floor or on your bed. Just be sure to keep good posture with your back straight.

Sitting on the floor

Strumming the Strings

To *strum* means to play the strings with your right hand by brushing quickly across them. There are two common ways of strumming the strings. One is with your fingers, and the other is with a pick.

Strumming with a Pick

Hold the pick between your thumb and index finger. Hold it firmly, but don't squeeze it too hard.

Strum from the sixth string (the thickest, lowest-sounding string) to the first string (the thinnest, highest-sounding string).

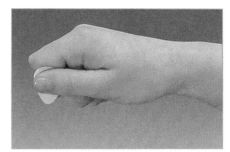

Start near the top string.

Move mostly your wrist, not just your arm. Finish near the bottom string.

Strumming with Your Fingers

First decide if you feel more comfortable strumming with the side of your thumb or the nail of your index finger. The strumming motion is the same with the thumb or finger as it is when using the pick. Strum from the sixth string (the thickest, lowest-sounding string) to the first string (the thinnest, highest-sounding string).

Strumming with the thumb

Strumming with the index finger

Important:

Strum by mostly moving your wrist, not just your arm. Use as little motion as possible. Start as close to the top string as you can, and never let your hand move past the edge of the guitar.

Time to Strum!

CD 1
Track 3

Strum all six strings slowly and evenly.

Count your strums out loud as you play.

Repeat this exercise until you feel comfortable strumming the strings.

strum	strum	strum	strum	strum	strum	strum	strum
/	/	/	/	/	/	/	/
Count: 1	2	3	4	5	6	7	8

Strumming Notation

Beats

Each strum you play is equal to one *beat*.
Beats are even, like the ticking of a clock.

tick - tick - tick - tick
beat-beat-beat-beat

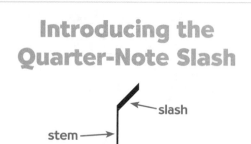
The Staff and Treble Clef

Guitar music is usually written on a five-line *staff* that has a *treble clef* at its beginning.

Treble clef

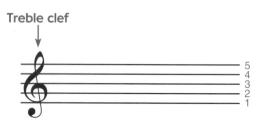

5
4
3
2
1

Bar Lines, Measures, and Time Signatures

Bar lines divide the staff into equal parts called measures. A *double bar line* is used at the end to show you the music is finished.

Bar lines   Double bar line

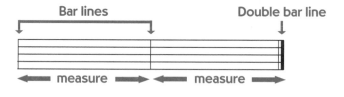

← measure →   ← measure →

Measures are always filled with a certain number of beats. You know how many beats are in each measure by looking at the *time signature*, which is always at the beginning of the music. A $\frac{4}{4}$ time signature ("four-four time") means there are 4 equal beats in every measure.

Time signature

CD 1
Track 4

More Time to Strum

Play this example in $\frac{4}{4}$ time. It will sound the same as "Time to Strum," which you played on the previous page. Keep the beats even and count out loud.

First time: Strum all six strings as you did before.

Strumming strings 3–2–1

Strum Strum Strum Strum   Strum Strum Strum Strum

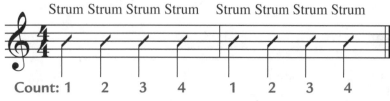

Count: 1   2   3   4   1   2   3   4

Second time: Strum starting with the third string, and strum only strings 3, 2, and 1.

ACTIVITY:
The Staff and Treble Clef

Guitar music is usually written on a five-line *staff*. The lines are numbered from the bottom up.

5
4
3
2
1

At the beginning of each staff is a *treble clef* that looks like this:

How to Draw the Treble Clef

Step 1:   Draw a circle under the staff and fill it in.

Step 2:   Draw a curved line (like the letter "u") that starts from the bottom of the circle and touches the bottom of the first line of the staff.

Step 3:   Draw a line up from the first line to the fifth line.

Step 4:   Draw a loop above the second line of the staff.

Step 5:   Draw a long curving line that goes around the second line of the staff.

Now, draw six treble clefs below.

11

ACTIVITY: Bar Lines and Measures

Bar lines divide the staff into equal parts called *measures*.
A *double bar line* is used at the end to show you the music is finished.

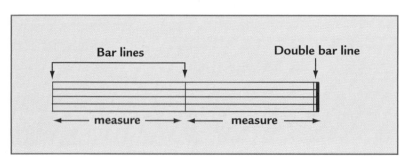

How to Draw Measures

Draw bar lines and a double bar line.

Draw the treble clef, bar lines, and double bar line to make four measures.

Make the same four measures again.

ACTIVITY:
The $\frac{4}{4}$ Time Signature

A *time signature* tells you how many beats are in a measure.
A $\frac{4}{4}$ time signature means there are four equal beats in every measure.

How to Draw the $\frac{4}{4}$ Time Signature

Step 1: Draw a number "4" sitting on top of the third line of the staff.

Step 2: Draw a second "4" below the first one, sitting on the bottom line.

Now, draw six $\frac{4}{4}$ time signatures.

ACTIVITY:
The Quarter-Note Slash

A slash with a stem is called a *quarter-note slash*.
Each quarter-note slash equals one beat.

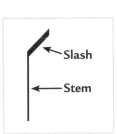

How to Draw the Quarter-Note Slash

Step 1: Create the slash by drawing a slanted line from the second staff line to the fourth staff line.

Step 2: Create the stem by drawing a line from the bottom of the slash to just below the staff.

Now, draw six quarter-note slashes.

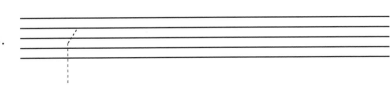

ACTIVITY: Counting Time

Draw four quarter-note slashes in each measure.

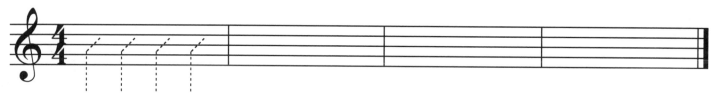

Write the counts for each measure below the quarter-note slashes.

Draw four measures including a treble clef, $\frac{4}{4}$ time signature, bar lines, a double bar line, and four quarter-note slashes in each measure. Then, write the counts below the measures.

Using Your Left Hand

Hand Position

Learning to use your left-hand fingers easily starts with a good hand position. Place your hand so your thumb rests comfortably in the middle of the back of the neck. Position your fingers on the front of the neck as if you are gently squeezing a ball between them and your thumb. Keep your elbow in and your fingers curved.

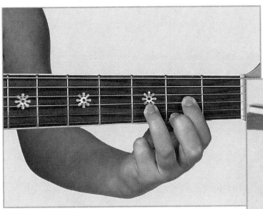

Keep elbow in and fingers curved

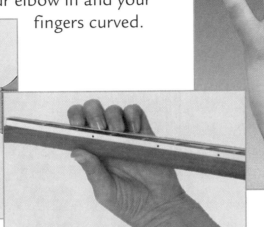

Like gently squeezing a ball between your fingertips and thumb

Placing a Finger on a String

When you press a string with a left-hand finger, make sure you press firmly with the tip of your finger and as close to the fret wire as you can without actually being right on it. Short fingernails are important! This will create a clean, bright tone.

RIGHT
Finger presses the string down near the fret without actually being on it.

WRONG
Finger is too far from fret wire; tone is "buzzy" and indefinite.

WRONG
Finger is on top of fret wire; tone is muffled and unclear.

How to Read Chord Diagrams

Chord diagrams show where to place your fingers. The example to the right shows finger 1 on the first string at the first fret. The Xs above the sixth, fifth and fourth strings tell you not to play them and only strum the third, second and first strings. Strings that are not played in a chord also look like dashed lines. The os above the second and third strings tell you these strings are to be played *open,* meaning without pressing down on them with a left-hand finger.

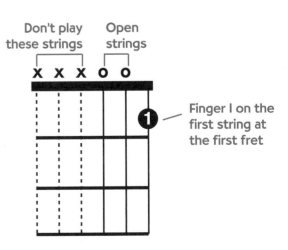

15

The Three-String C Chord

Use finger 1 to press the 2nd string at the 1st fret.
Strum strings 3–2–1.

C

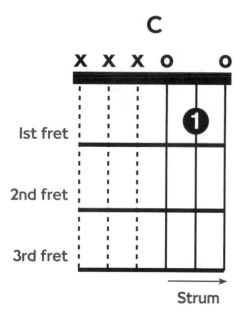

My First Chord
CD 1
Track 6

Strumming

Strum the three-string C chord on each quarter-note slash ⸺. Make sure your strums are even. Count aloud as you play:

1–2–3–4 | 1–2–3–4.

Listen to the song on your CD to hear how it should sound!

Remember: This means there are 4 beats in each measure.

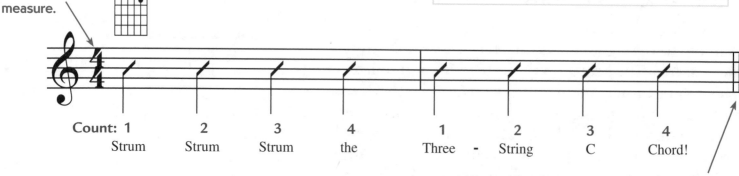

Count: 1   2   3   4   1   2   3   4
Strum   Strum   Strum   the   Three - String   C   Chord!

This **double bar line** tells us the music is finished.

ACTIVITY:
The Three-String C Chord

Chord Diagrams

When reading a chord diagram, you will see exactly where to put your fingers. Each vertical line represents one of the six strings of the guitar: from left to right, 6 5 4 3 2 1. An **x** above a string means do not play it, and sometimes that string will also be shown as a dashed line. An **o** above a string means it is played open (not fingered). A circled number on a string shows you which finger to use and where to place it on that string.

Three-String C Chord

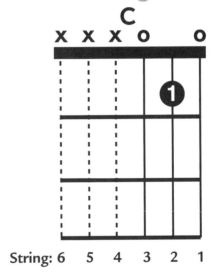

String: 6 5 4 3 2 1

Write the chord symbol "C" three times.

Draw the **x**'s, **o**'s, and fingering for the three-string C chords below.

C

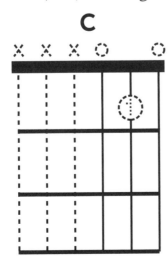

C

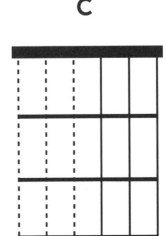

The Quarter Rest

Introducing the Quarter Rest

This strange-looking music symbol means to be silent for one beat. Stop the sound of the strings by lightly touching them with the side of your hand, as in the photo.

1 beat

CD 1
Track 7

Rest Warm-up

Before playing "Three Blind Mice," practice this exercise until you are comfortable playing rests.

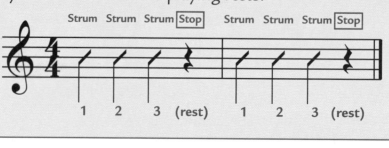

Strum Strum Strum Stop   Strum Strum Strum Stop

1   2   3   (rest)   1   2   3   (rest)

Practice Tip

Strum the chords and have a friend sing the words.

Three Blind Mice

CD 1
Track 8

C
xxx o o

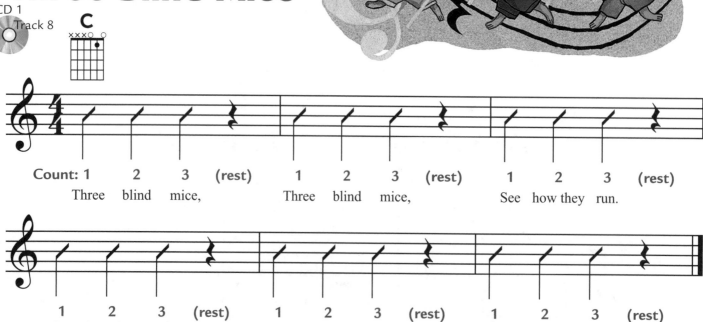

Count: 1   2   3   (rest)   1   2   3   (rest)   1   2   3   (rest)
Three blind mice,   Three blind mice,   See how they run.

1   2   3   (rest)   1   2   3   (rest)   1   2   3   (rest)
See how they run.   Three blind mice,   Three blind mice.

18

ACTIVITY: The Quarter Rest

The *quarter rest* means to be silent for one beat.

Quarter Rest

How to Draw the Quarter Rest

Step 1: Draw a short line slanting down from left to right.

Step 2: Draw a longer line slanting down from right to left starting at the bottom of the first line.

Step 3: Draw another short line slanting down from left to right starting at the bottom of the second line.

Step 4: Draw a curled line, almost like a letter "c," starting at the bottom of the third line.

Now, draw five quarter rests.

Counting Time

Fill in the missing beats with quarter rests.

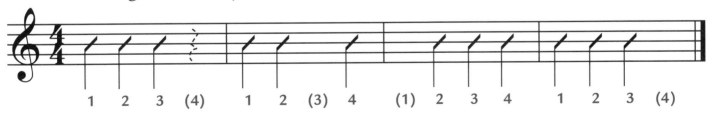

1	2	3	(4)	1	2	(3)	4	(1)	2	3	4	1	2	3	(4)

Write the counts below the staff. Put parentheses around the counts that are for rests.

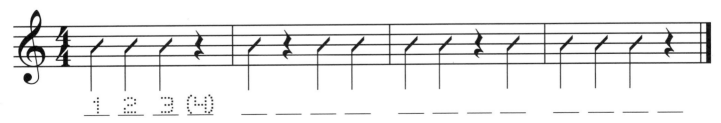

1 2 3 (4) __ __ __ __ __ __ __ __ __ __ __ __

19

The Three-String G⁷ Chord

Hear this chord!
CD 1
Track 9

Use finger 1 to press the 1st string at the 1st fret.
Strum strings 3–2–1.

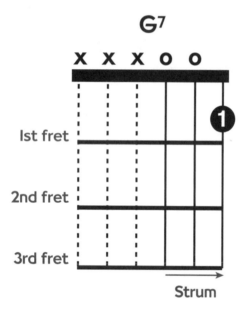

My Second Chord

CD 1
Track 10

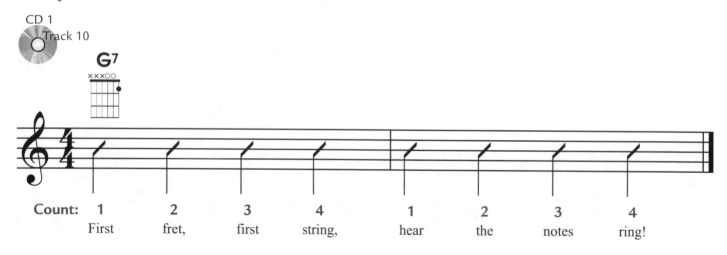

Count:	1	2	3	4	1	2	3	4
	First	fret,	first	string,	hear	the	notes	ring!

ACTIVITY:
The Three-String G⁷ Chord

Three-String G⁷ Chord

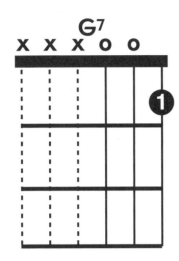

Finish drawing the **x**'s, **o**'s, and fingering for the chord below.

Write the chord symbol "G⁷" three times.

G⁷
_____

_____

Troubadour Song

Remember to stop the sound by lightly touching the strings with the side of your hand on each 𝄾. Wait one beat.

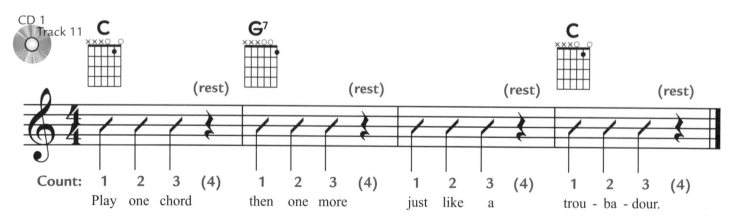

*A troubadour was a musician who traveled around singing and playing.

Skip to My Lou

Practice Tip

To change quickly from G⁷ to C in the last two measures, just move your finger from the 1st string to the 2nd string—that's not very far.

G⁷   C

CD 1
Track 12

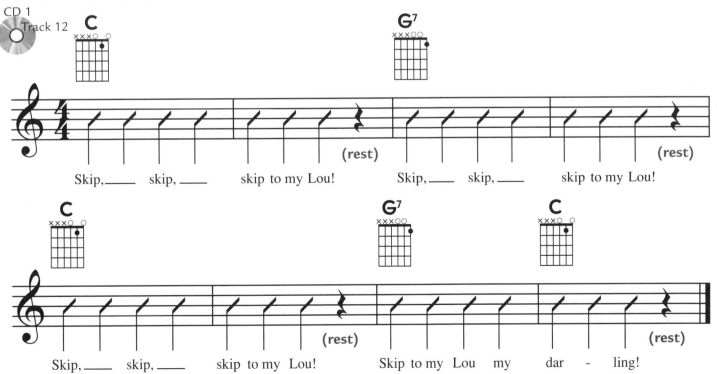

Skip,___ skip,___ skip to my Lou! Skip,___ skip,___ skip to my Lou!

Skip,___ skip,___ skip to my Lou! Skip to my Lou my dar - ling!

23

London Bridge

C **G⁷** **C**

Lon - don Bridge is   fal - ling down, (rest)   fal - ling down, (rest)   fal - ling down (rest)

(No new chord symbol, so keep playing C!)

G⁷ **C**

Lon - don Bridge is   fal - ling down, (rest)   my____ fair____   la - dy. (rest)

Remember to move first finger
quickly back to the 2nd string to
play the C chord on the next beat.

24

The Three-String G Chord

Hear this chord!
CD 1
Track 14

Use finger 3 to press the 1st string at the 3rd fret.
Strum strings 3–2–1.

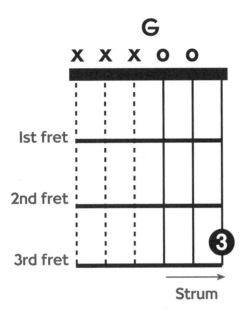

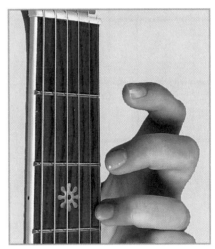

My Third Chord

CD 1
Track 15

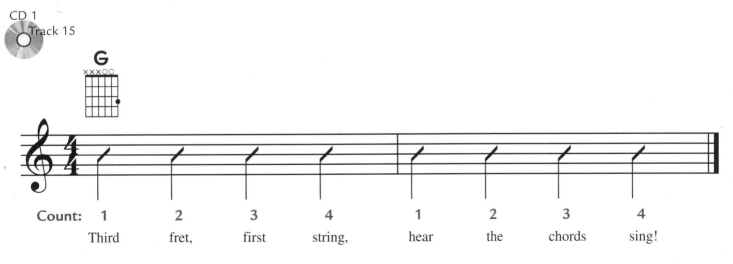

Count: 1   2   3   4   1   2   3   4
Third   fret,   first   string, hear   the   chords   sing!

ACTIVITY:
The Three-String G Chord

26

Three-String G Chord

G

x x x o o

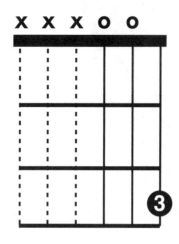

Finish drawing the **x**'s, **o**'s, and fingering for the chord below.

G

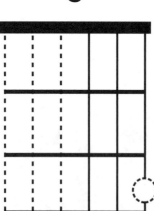

Write the chord symbol
"G" three times.

G

_____

_____

Three Chords in One Song

C

G⁷

G
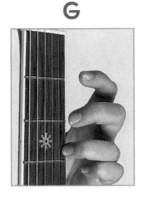

Remember:

This song has three different chords in it. At first, take your time and play slowly so that all the notes sound clearly. Don't forget to be silent for a beat on each quarter rest as you change to a new chord.

Rain Comes Down

CD 1
Track 16

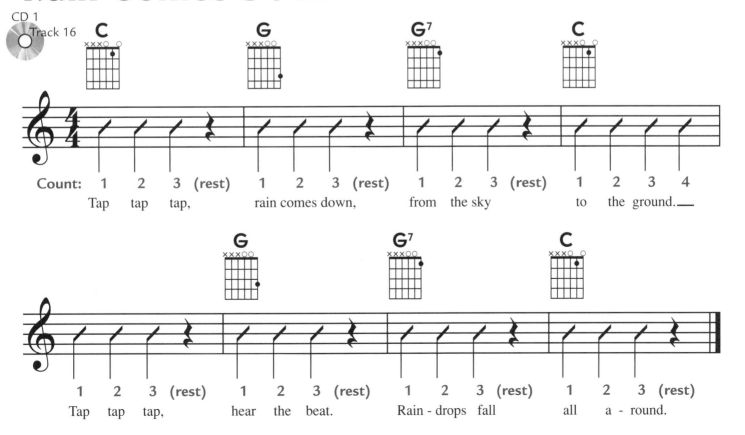

Count: 1 2 3 (rest)   1 2 3 (rest)   1 2 3 (rest)   1 2 3 4

Tap tap tap,   rain comes down,   from the sky   to the ground. ___

1 2 3 (rest)   1 2 3 (rest)   1 2 3 (rest)   1 2 3 (rest)

Tap tap tap,   hear the beat.   Rain-drops fall   all a-round.

The Repeat Sign

Introducing the Repeat Sign :|

Double dots on the inside of a double bar line mean to go back to the beginning and play again.

Merrily We Roll Along

CD 1
Track 17

C | G | C

Mer - ri - ly we roll a - long, roll a - long, roll a - long.

G7 | C

Repeat from the beginning

Mer - ri - ly we roll a - long ____ o'er the deep blue sea. ____

28

ACTIVITY: The Repeat Sign

When *double dots* are written on the inside of a double bar line, it makes a *repeat sign*. A repeat sign means to go back to the beginning and play the same music again.

How to Draw the Repeat Sign

Draw repeat signs by adding double dots to these double bar lines.

Draw a double bar line above each "Don't Repeat," and draw a repeat sign above each "Repeat."

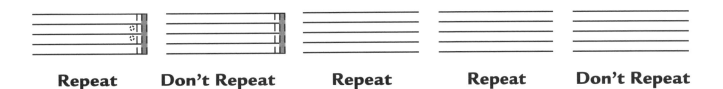

Repeat **Don't Repeat** **Repeat** **Repeat** **Don't Repeat**

Love Somebody

CD 1
Track 18

C
1. Love some-bod - y, yes I do! —— Love some-bod - y, won't say who. ——
2. Love some-bod - y, want to hear? —— Let me whis - per in your ear. ——

C
Love some-bod - y, can you guess? —— Who's the one that I love best?
Love some-bod - y, now you've guessed —— You're the one that I love best!

The Three-String D⁷ Chord

Hear this chord!
CD 1
Track 19

Use finger 1 to press the 2nd string at the 1st fret. Use fingers 2 and 3 to press the 3rd and 1st strings at the 2nd fret. Strum strings 3–2–1.

D⁷

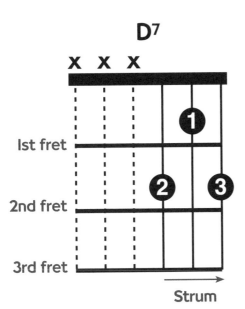

My Fourth Chord

CD 1
Track 20

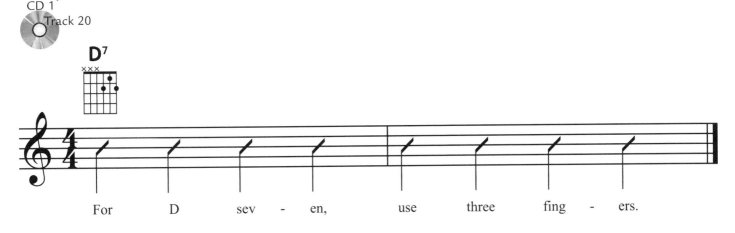

For   D   sev - en,   use   three   fing - ers.

31

ACTIVITY: The Three-String D⁷ Chord

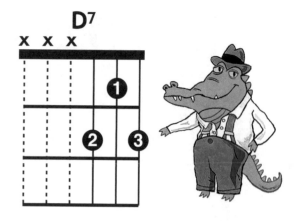

D7

x x x

Write the chord symbol "D⁷" three times.

D7 _____ _____

Draw the **x**'s and **o**'s for these chords.

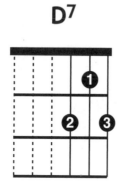 D7

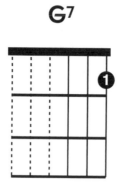 G7

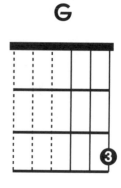 G

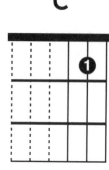 C

Let's Practice Writing Music

Finish creating four measures of music by tracing the treble clefs, time signature, bar lines, quarter-note slashes, quarter rests, repeat sign, and chord frames.

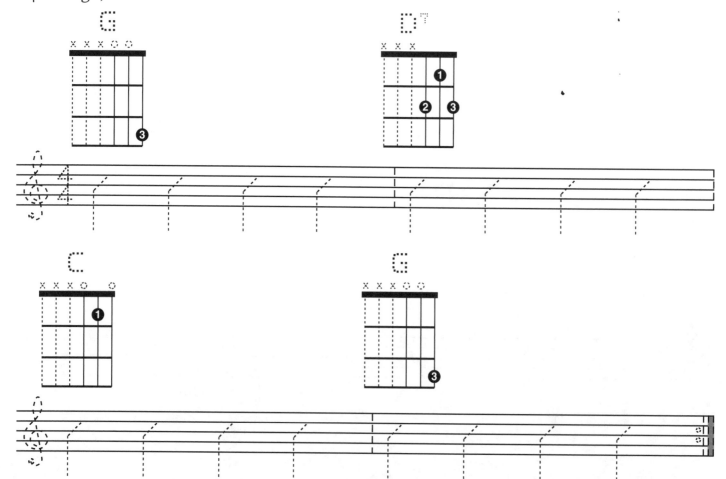

Using D⁷ with Other Chords

Practice Tip

Before you play "When the Saints Go Marching In" and "Yankee Doodle," practice the exercises on this page. They will help you to change chords easily.

Play each exercise very slowly at first, and gradually play them faster. Don't move on to the songs until you can easily move from chord to chord without missing a beat.

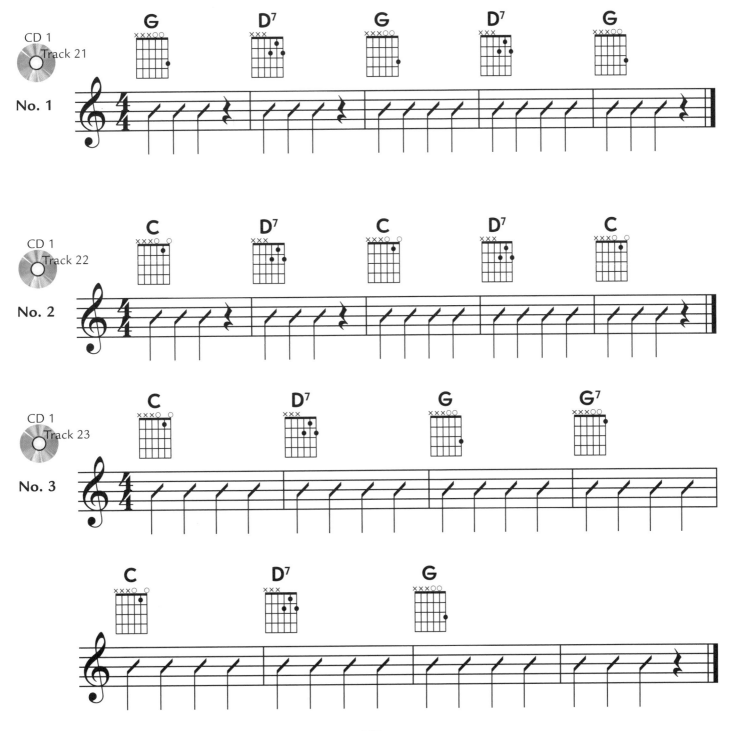

When the Saints Go Marching In

Yankee Doodle

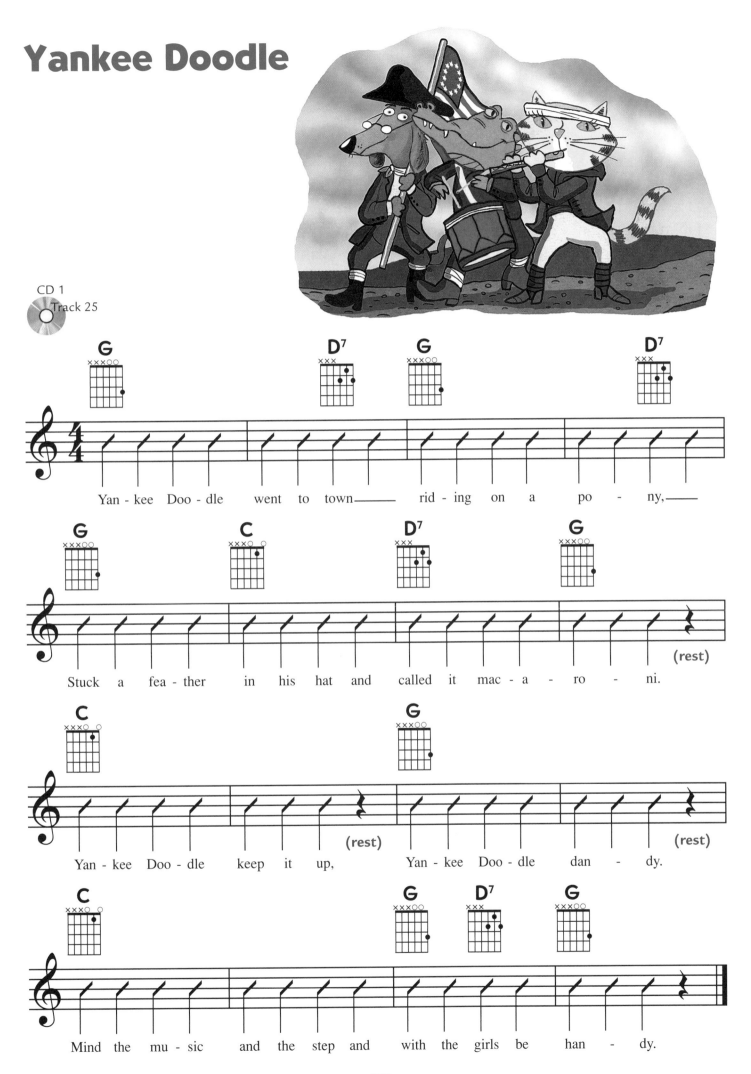

CD 1
Track 25

G   **D⁷**   **G**   **D⁷**

Yan - kee Doo - dle   went to town——   rid - ing on a   po - ny,——

G   **C**   **D⁷**   **G**

Stuck a fea - ther   in his hat and called it mac - a - ro - ni.   (rest)

C   **G**

Yan - kee Doo - dle   keep it up, (rest)   Yan - kee Doo - dle   dan - dy. (rest)

C   **G** **D⁷** **G**

Mind the mu - sic   and the step and   with the girls be   han - dy.

35

ACTIVITY: Write Your Own Song With Three-String Chords

Here's your chance to write your first song. Follow these steps.

1. Draw a treble clef at the beginning of each staff.
2. Draw a $\frac{4}{4}$ time signature next to the treble clef in the first measure.
3. Fill in the bar lines and draw a repeat sign at the end.
4. Draw quarter-note slashes and quarter rests. You can choose which beats have slashes and which have rests, but be sure there are exactly four beats in each measure.
5. Choose which chords you want by filling in the chord frame above each measure.
6. Make up your own lyrics and write them below each staff.
7. **Have fun** and play your song on your guitar.

Getting Acquainted with Music Notation

Notes

Musical sounds are represented by symbols called *notes*. Their time value is determined by their color (black or white), and by stems and flags attached to them.

The Staff

Each note has a name. That name depends on where the note is found on the *staff*. The staff is made up of five horizontal lines and the spaces between those lines.

```
——————————————— 5th LINE ———————————————
                                           4th SPACE
—————————— 4th LINE ——————————
                                 3rd SPACE
————— 3rd LINE —————
                       2nd SPACE
——— 2nd LINE ———
              1st SPACE
— 1st LINE ———————————————
```

The Music Alphabet

The notes are named after the first seven letters of the alphabet (A–G).

A   B   C   D   E   F   G

Clefs

As music notation progressed through history, the staff had from two to twenty lines, and symbols were invented that would always give you a reference point for all the other notes. These symbols were called *clefs*.

Music for the guitar is written in the *G* or *treble clef*. Originally, the Gothic letter G was used on a four-line staff to show the pitch G.

This developed into the modern clef:

ACTIVITY:
The Staff

The *staff* is made up of five horizontal lines and the four spaces between those lines. The lines and spaces are numbered from the bottom up.

```
———————————————————— 5th LINE ————————————————
                                                    4th SPACE
——————————————— 4th LINE ——————————————
                                      3rd SPACE
————————— 3rd LINE —————————
                             2nd SPACE
—————— 2nd LINE ——————
                      1st SPACE
— 1st LINE ——————————————————
```

Name the line or space for each note.

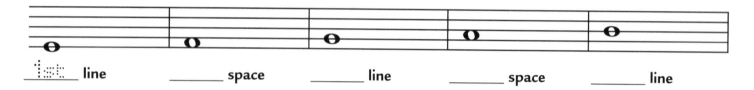

_1st_ line   _____ space   _____ line   _____ space   _____ line

_____ space   _____ line   _____ space   _____ line

Name the line for each note in the box below the staff.

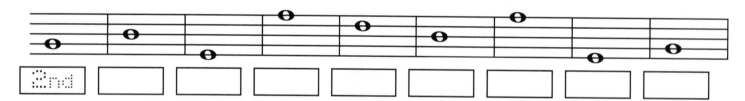

2nd								

Name the space for each note in the box below the staff.

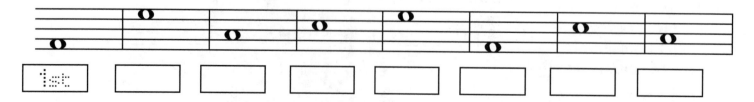

1st							

38

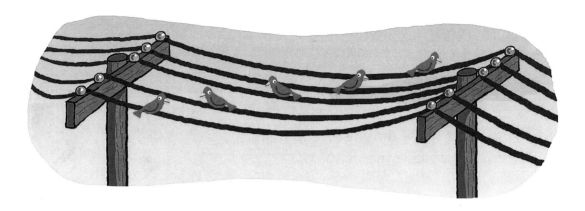

An easy way to remember the notes on the lines is using the phrase **E**very **G**ood **B**ird **D**oes **F**ly. Remembering the notes in the spaces is even easier because they spell the word **FACE**, which rhymes with "space."

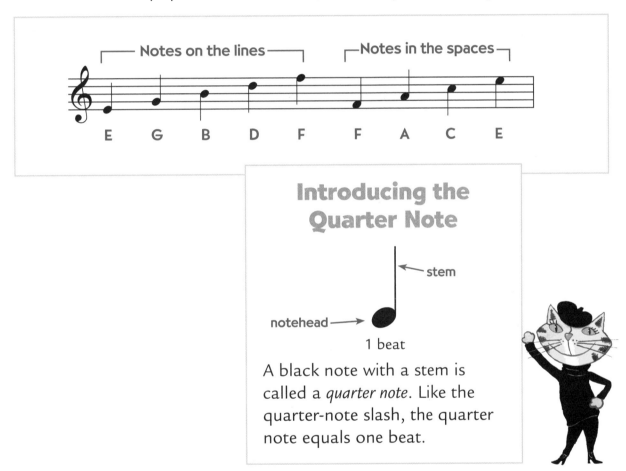

Introducing the Quarter Note

stem

notehead →

1 beat

A black note with a stem is called a *quarter note*. Like the quarter-note slash, the quarter note equals one beat.

CD 1
Track 26

Clap and Count out Loud

$\frac{4}{4}$

| 1 | 2 | 3 | 4 | 1 | 2 | 3 | (4) | 1 | 2 | 3 | (4) | 1 | 2 | 3 | (4) |

ACTIVITY: The Quarter Note

A *quarter note* has a black notehead and a stem. Each quarter note equals one beat.

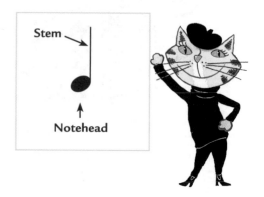

How to Draw the Quarter Note

Step 1: To create the notehead, draw an oval and fill it in. Draw several noteheads below in the third space.

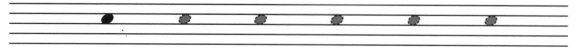

Step 2: To create the stem, draw a line going down from the left of the notehead to just below the staff.

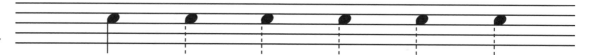

Now, draw six quarter notes on the third space of the staff.

Now, draw six quarter notes in the second space with the stem going up from the right of the notehead.

Counting Time

Draw four quarter notes in each measure. In the first two measures, draw quarter notes having stems down, and in the second two measures, draw quarter notes having stems up. Then, write the counts below the staff.

Notes on the First String
Introducing E

A note sitting on the top space of the treble clef staff is called E. To play this note, pick the *open* 1st string (meaning without putting a left-hand finger on it).

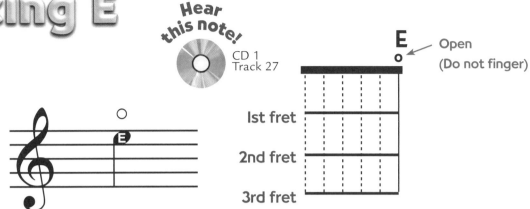

Hear this note!
CD 1 Track 27

E — Open (Do not finger)

1st fret
2nd fret
3rd fret

Elizabeth, the Elephant

CD 1 Track 28

Picking

- Play each E slowly and evenly, using a *downpick* motion. We will use only downpicks for the rest of the book.
- Use only a little motion to pick each note, just like strumming.

Count: 1 2 3 4   1 2 3 4   1 2 3 4   1 2 3 4
El - e - phants eat   en - chil - a - das,   es - pe - cial - ly   E - li - za - beth.

ACTIVITY: The Note E (1st String)

The note on the top space of the staff is called E.

Drawing the Note E

Step 1: Draw an oval notehead in the top space of the staff.

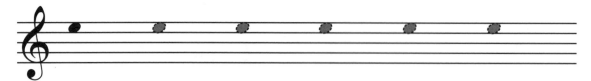

Step 2: For the stem, draw a line from the left of the notehead to the bottom space of the staff. The stem always goes down for this note.

Now, draw the note E six times below.

Playing the Note E

To play the note E, pick the open 1st string.

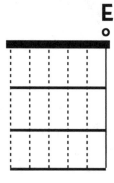

Indicate the fingering for note E by placing "**o**" above the 1st string on each diagram.

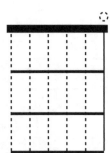
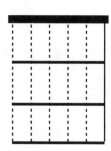
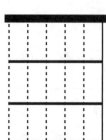

The Note E with Chords

Practice Tip

For this tune, notice that both the C and G⁷ chords are fingered with finger 1 at the first fret.

C Chord

G⁷ Chord

Simply move your finger over one string to change chords.

CD 1
Track 29

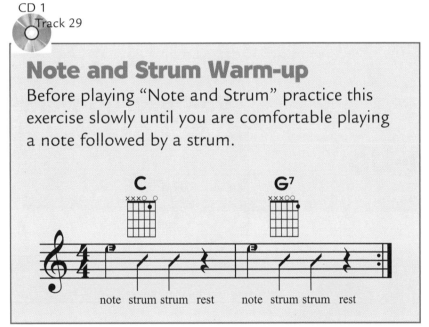

Note and Strum Warm-up
Before playing "Note and Strum" practice this exercise slowly until you are comfortable playing a note followed by a strum.

Note and Strum

CD 1
Track 30

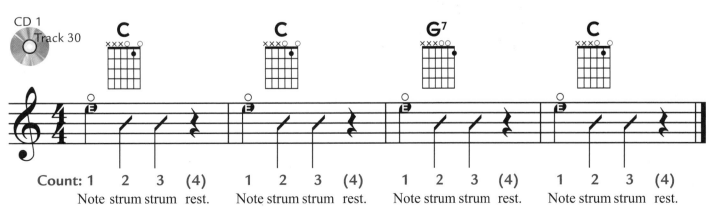

Notes on the First String
Introducing F

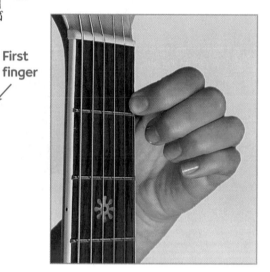

A note on the top line of the staff is called F. To play this note, use finger 1 to press the 1st string at the 1st fret. Use a down-pick motion to play only the 1st string.

Hear this note!
CD 1
Track 31

F

First finger

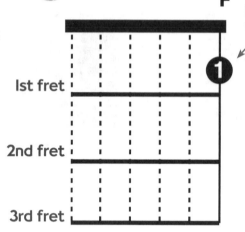

1st fret
2nd fret
3rd fret

Up-Down-Up

CD 1
Track 33

CD 1
Track 32

Up-Down-Up Warm-up

Before playing "Up-Down-Up," practice this exercise until you are comfortable playing the note F.

Start on E then up, first fin-ger. Down to E then up to the F.

ACTIVITY:
The Note F (1st String)

The note on the top line of the staff is called F.

Drawing the Note F

Drawing the note F is similar to drawing the note E, except the note-head is on the top line. On the staff below, draw the note F six times.

Playing the Note F

To play the note F, press the 1st string at the 1st fret.

F

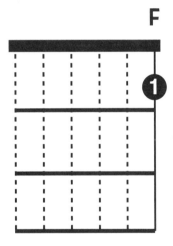

On the diagram to the right, indicate the fingering for the note F by placing the number "1" in a circle on the 1st fret of the 1st string.

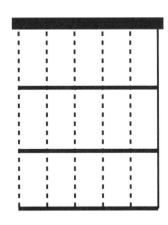

The Notes E and F with Chords

Practice Tip

For this tune, notice that the note F and the G^7 chord are both fingered with finger 1 at the 1st fret on the 1st string.

Note F   **G^7 Chord**

Don't lift your 1st finger between the note F and the G^7 chord.

CD 1
Track 34

Hold down lst finger

E strum strum rest.   F strum strum rest.   One more time rest,   then you can rest.

46

Notes on the First String
Introducing G

Hear this note! CD 1 Track 35

A note on the space above the staff is called G. Use finger 3 to press the 1st string at the 3rd fret. Use a downpick motion to play only the 1st string.

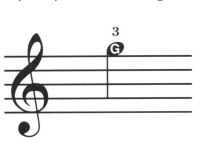

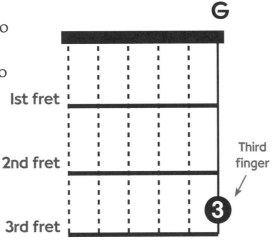

G

1st fret

2nd fret

Third finger

3rd fret

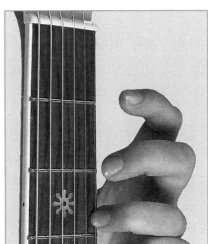

CD 1 Track 36

G Warm-up

The Mountain Climber

CD 1 Track 37

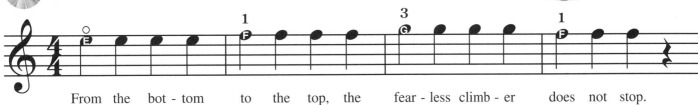

From the bot - tom   to the top, the   fear - less climb - er   does not stop.

With his   pick and   tuned gui - tar, the   pre - pared climb - er   will go   far.

ACTIVITY:
The Note G (1st String)

The note on the space above the staff is called G.

Drawing the Note G

To draw the note G on the staff, place the notehead on the space above the staff, and draw the stem down to the second line. On the staff below, draw the note G six times.

Playing the Note G

To play the note G, press the 1st string at the 3rd fret.

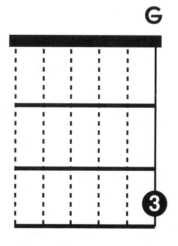

On the diagram to the right, indicate the fingering for the note G by placing the number "3" in a circle on the 3rd fret of the 1st string.

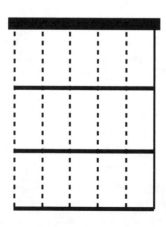

The Notes E, F, and G with Chords

Practice Tip

Notice that the note G and the G chord are both fingered with finger 3 at the 3rd fret on the 1st string.

Note G

G Chord

Hold down the 3rd finger between the notes G and the G chord.

Brave in the Cave

CD 1
Track 38

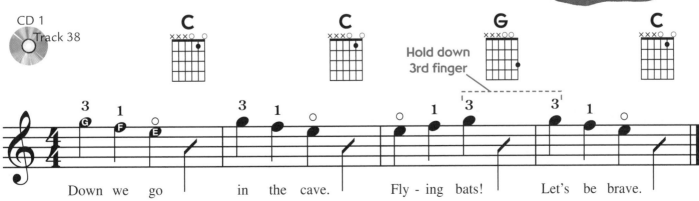

C   C   G   C

Hold down 3rd finger

Down we go   in the cave.   Fly - ing bats!   Let's be brave.

49

Single Notes, Then Chord! Chord! Chord!

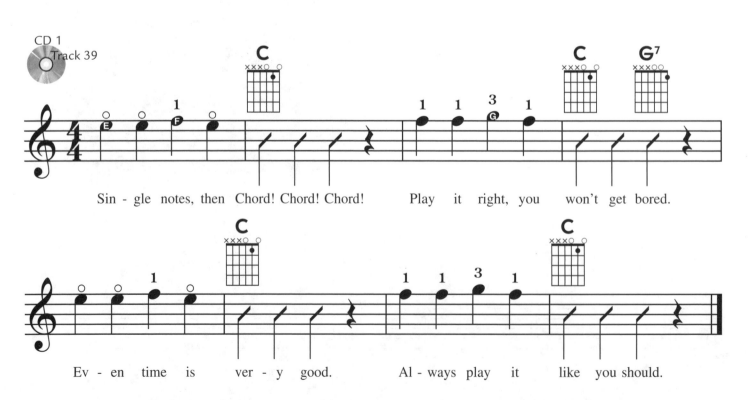

Pumpkin Song

G⁷

C

Can - dle in his head. Doesn't need to be fed.

G⁷

C

Makes a tas - ty pie. Seeds help witch - es fly!

51

Notes on the Second String
Introducing B

Hear this note!
CD 1
Track 41

A note on the middle line of the staff is called B. Play the 2nd string open.

B — Open

1st fret
2nd fret
3rd fret

CD 1
Track 42

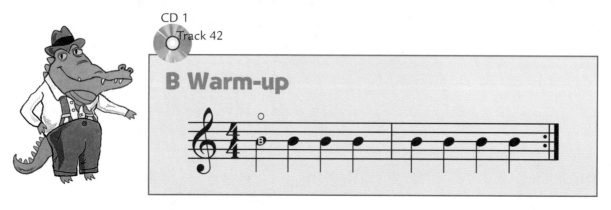

B Warm-up

Two Open Strings

CD 1
Track 43

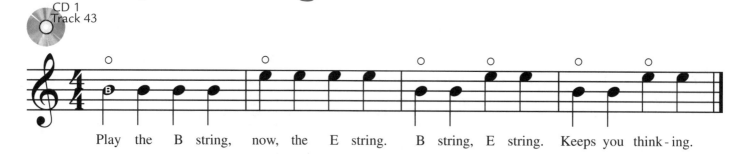

Play the B string, now, the E string. B string, E string. Keeps you think-ing.

Two-String Melody

CD 1
Track 44

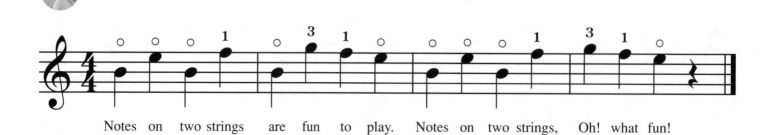

Notes on two strings are fun to play. Notes on two strings, Oh! what fun!

ACTIVITY:
The Note B (2nd String)

The note on the third line of the staff is called B.

Drawing the Note B

To draw the note B on the staff, place the notehead on the third line, and draw the stem down to just below the staff. On the staff below, draw the note B six times.

Playing the Note B

To play the note B, press the open 2nd string.

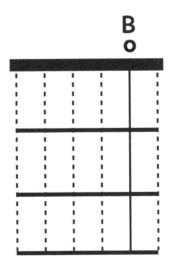

On the diagram to the right, indicate the fingering for the note B by placing "o" above the 2nd string.

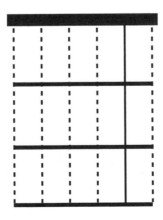

Jumping Around

CD 1
Track 45

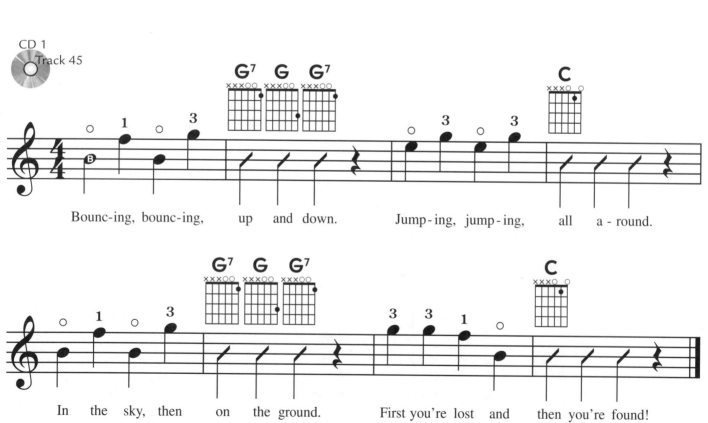

Bounc-ing, bounc-ing,   up   and down.   Jump-ing, jump-ing,   all a - round.

In   the   sky, then   on   the ground.   First you're lost and   then you're found!

54

Notes on the Second String
Introducing C

Hear this note!

CD 1
Track 46

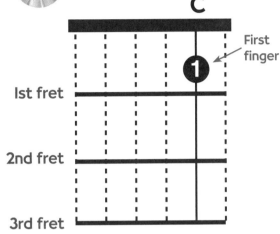

C

First finger

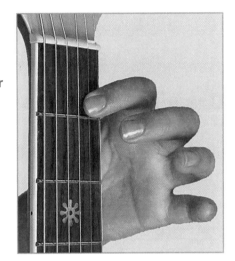

A note on the 3rd space of the staff is called C. Use finger 1 to press the 2nd string at the 1st fret. Pick only the 2nd string.

Ist fret

2nd fret

3rd fret

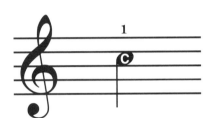

CD 1
Track 47

C Warm-up

Ping Pong Song

CD 1
Track 48

O - pen B string, first fin - ger C, down to B then up to C.

Soccer Game

CD 1
Track 49

Hold

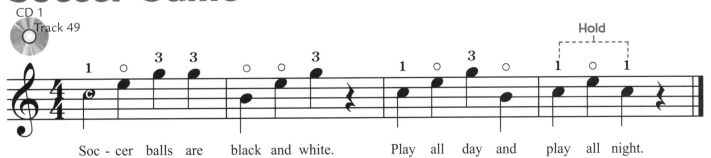

Soc - cer balls are black and white. Play all day and play all night.

ACTIVITY: The Note C (2nd String)

The note on the third space of the staff is called C.

Drawing the Note C

To draw the note C on the staff, place the notehead on the third space, and draw the stem down to just below the staff. On the staff below, draw the note C six times.

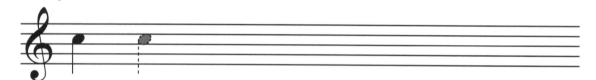

Playing the Note C

To play the note C, press the 2nd string at the 1st fret.

C

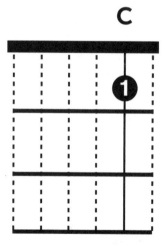

On the diagram to the right, indicate the fingering for the note C by placing the number "1" in a circle on the 1st fret of the 2nd string.

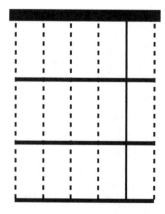

The Half Rest

Introducing the Half Rest

This rest means do not play for two beats,

which is the same as 𝄾 𝄾 .

 CD 1
Track 50

Clap and Count out Loud

| | | | | | | | (rest) | (rest) | | | (rest) | | (rest) | (rest) | (rest) | | |
| 1 | 2 | 3 | 4 | 1 | 2 | (3) | (4) | 1 | (2) | 3 | (4) | (1) | (2) | 3 | 4 |

Practice Tip

Notice that the note C and the D⁷ chord are both fingered with finger 1 at the 1st fret on the 2nd string.

In "When I Feel Best," hold the 1st finger down from the third beat of the 1st measure until the last beat of the 5th measure.

Note C

D⁷ Chord

When I Feel Best

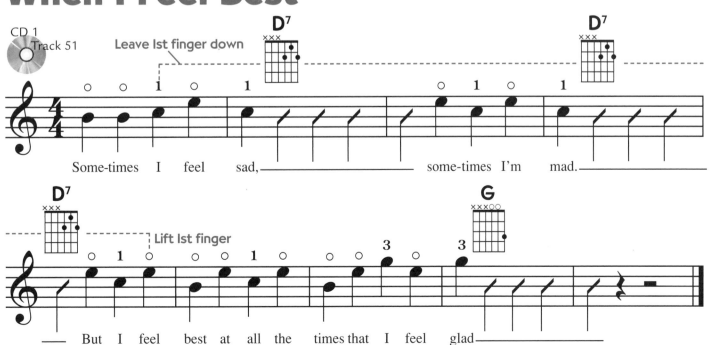

Some-times I feel sad,_____ some-times I'm mad._____

_____ But I feel best at all the times that I feel glad_____

57

ACTIVITY: The Half Rest

A *half rest* means do not play for two beats.

How to Draw the Half Rest

Step 1: Draw a box on top of the middle line of the staff.

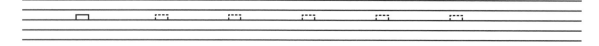

Step 2: Fill in the box.

Now, draw six half rests.

Notes on the Second String
Introducing D

Hear this note! CD 1 Track 52

A note on the 4th line of the staff is called D. Use finger 3 to press the 2nd string at the 3rd fret. Pick only the 2nd string.

D

1st fret

2nd fret

3rd fret

3 — Third finger

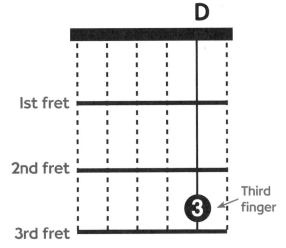

CD 1 Track 53

D Warm-up

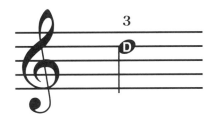

A-Choo!

CD 1 Track 54

B and C and D are eas - y. Spil - ling pep - per makes me sneez - y.

"A - a - choo! A - a - choo!" Pep - per makes me go "A - choo!"

59

ACTIVITY:
The Note D (2nd String)

The note on the fourth line of the staff is called D.

Drawing the Note D

To draw the note D on the staff, place the notehead on the fourth line, and draw the stem down to just below the staff. On the staff below, draw the note D six times.

Playing the Note D

To play the note D, press the 2nd string at the 3rd fret.

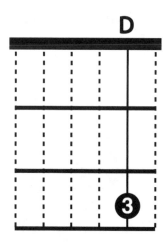

On the diagram to the right, indicate the fingering for the note D by placing the number "3" in a circle on the 3rd fret of the 2nd string.

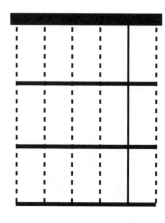

ACTIVITY:
The Notes B, C, D, E, F, and G

Reading the Notes B, C, D, E, F, and G

Write the letter name of each note in the box below the staff.

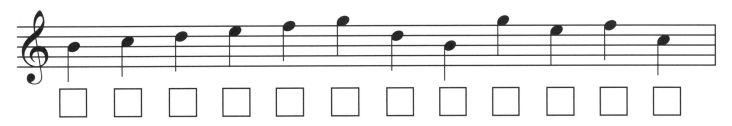

Word Fun with Notes

Write the letter name of each note on the line below the
staff. The notes in each measure spell a word!

Drawing the Notes B, C, D, E, F, and G

Write the noteheads first, and then add the stems going down.

Now, write all six notes in order from B to G two times.

ACTIVITY: Notes on the Strings: B, C, D, E, F, and G

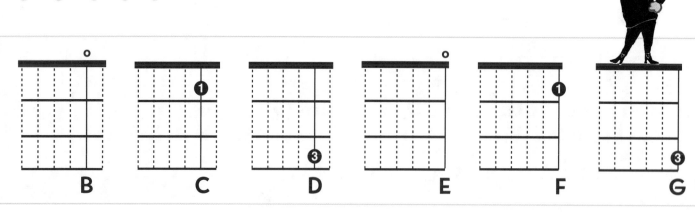

Write the correct note name below each fingered string.

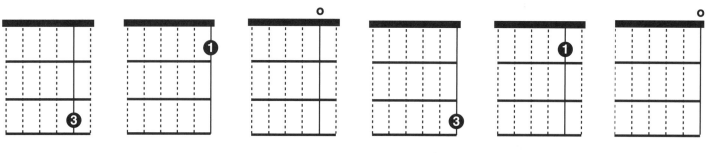

Draw the note on the staff above each note name. Use quarter notes.

C   E   G   B   D   F

Draw the fingering on the fretboard diagram above each note.

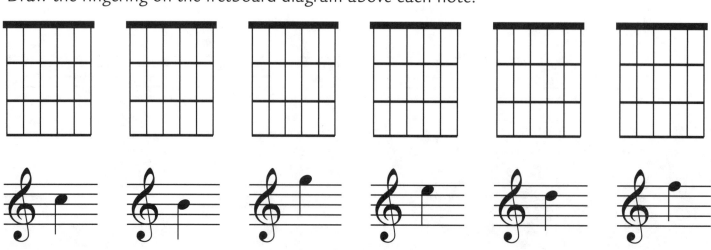

The Half Note

2 beats

This note lasts two beats.
It is twice as long as a quarter note.

CD 1
Track 55

Clap and Count out Loud

4/4

1 2 3 4   1 2 3 4   1 2 3 4   1 2 3 4

CD 1
Track 56

Ode to Joy
from Beethoven's 9th Symphony

Ludwig van Beethoven

Count: 1 2 3 4   1 2 3 4   1 2 3 4   1 2 3 4

When Bee-tho-ven wrote this tune he could not hear a sin-gle note.

Keep counting! But his mus-ic is so awe-some peo-ple still love things he wrote.

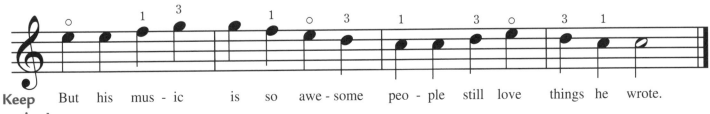

63

 ACTIVITY:
The Half Note

A *half note* lasts two beats. It is twice as long as a quarter note.

How to Draw the Half Note

Step 1: Create the notehead by drawing an oval. On the staff below, draw three noteheads in the third space and three noteheads in the second space.

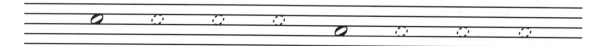

Step 2: Create the stems. For the first three notes, draw the stem going down from the left of the notehead, and for the second three notes, draw the stem going up from the right of the notehead.

Now, draw six half notes. Draw three on the third space, and three on the second space.

Counting Time

Fill in the missing beats by adding either a half rest or a half note in each measure. Then, write the counts below the staff. Put parentheses around beats that are for rests.

Jingle Bells

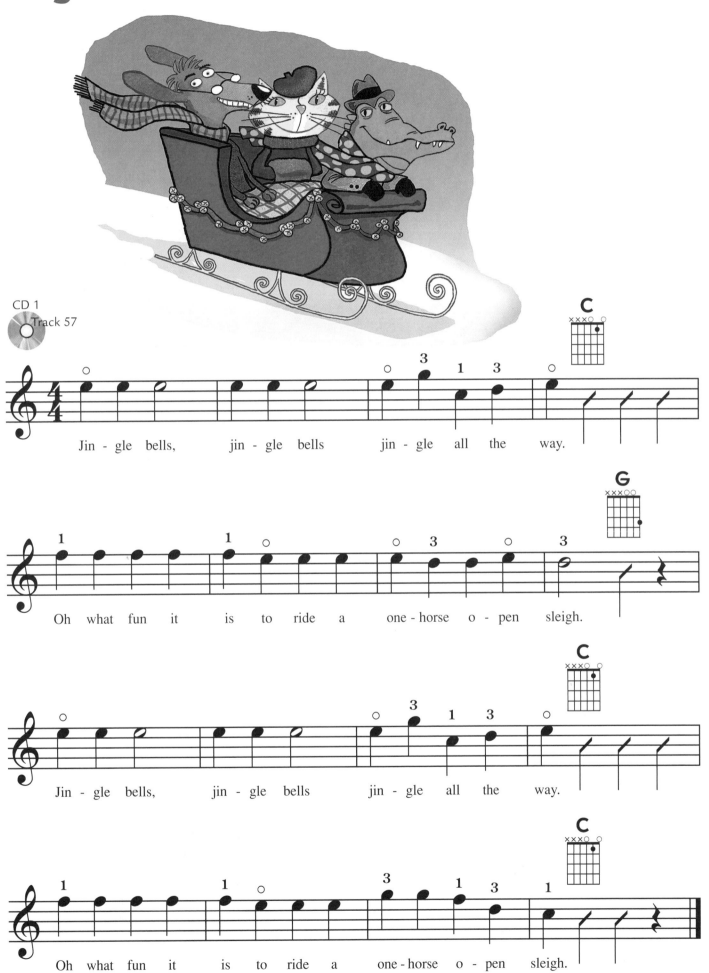

CD 1
Track 57

C

Jin - gle bells,   jin - gle bells   jin - gle all the way.

G

Oh what fun it   is to ride a   one - horse o - pen sleigh.

C

Jin - gle bells,   jin - gle bells   jin - gle all the way.

C

Oh what fun it   is to ride a   one - horse o - pen sleigh.

Mary Had a Little Lamb

CD 1
Track 58

G

Ma - ry had a lit - tle lamb, lit - tle lamb, lit - tle lamb,

C

Ma - ry had a lit - tle lamb, its fleece was white as snow.

G

Ev - 'ry - where that Ma - ry went, Ma - ry went, Ma - ry went,

C

Ev - 'ry - where that Ma - ry went, the lamb was sure to go.

Notes on the Third String
Introducing G

CD 1
Track 59

A note on the 2nd line of the staff is called G. Pick the 3rd string open.

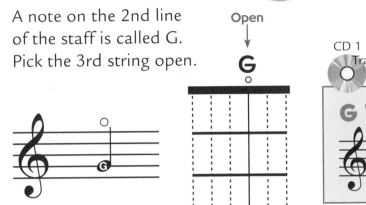

CD 1
Track 60

Three Open Strings

CD 1
Track 61

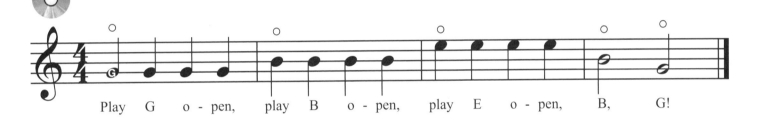

Play   G   o - pen,   play   B   o - pen,   play   E   o - pen,   B,   G!

Little Steps and Big Leaps

CD 1
Track 62

Play - ing   on   three   strings   lets   me   play   notes   far   a - part.

Lit - tle   steps   and   big   leaps   make   my   play - ing   like   fine   art.

ACTIVITY: The Note G (3rd String)

Drawing the Note G

To draw the note G on the staff, write the notehead first, and then add the stem going up.

Now, draw G on the staff once as a quarter note, then as a half note.

Quarter Note   **Half Note**

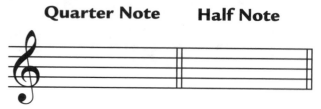

Playing the Note G

To play the note G, pick the open 3rd string.

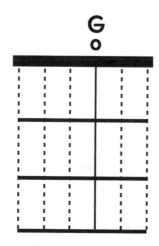

On the diagram to the right, indicate the fingering for the note G by placing "**o**" above the 3rd string.

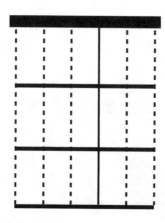

Alouette

Notes on the Third String
Introducing A

CD 1
Track 64

A note on the 2nd space of the staff is called A. Use finger 2 to press the 3rd string at the 2nd fret. Pick only the third string.

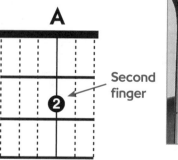

A

Second finger

CD 1
Track 65

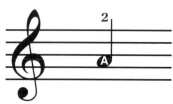

A Warm-up

Introducing the Whole Note

This note lasts four beats. It is as long as two half notes, or four quarter notes.

𝅝
4 beats

CD 1
Track 66

Clap and Count out Loud

𝄴 ♩ ♩ ♩ ♩ | 𝅝 | 𝅗𝅥 ♩ ♩ | 𝅝 ‖
1 2 3 4   1 2 3 4   1 2 3 4   1 2 3 4

CD 1
Track 67

A Is Easy!

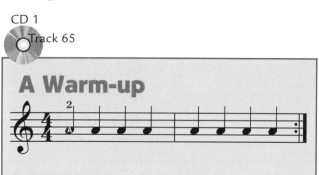

A is eas - y if you place your sec - ond fin - ger on the G string.

Taking a Walk

CD 1
Track 68

Walk - ing up to D, then walk down to G.

D⁷

G

Then I add some chords so I don't get bored.

70

ACTIVITY: The Note A (3rd String)

Drawing the Note A

To draw the note A on the staff, write the note-head first, and then add the stem going up.

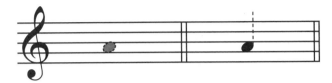

Playing the Note A

To play the note A, press the 3rd string at the 2nd fret.

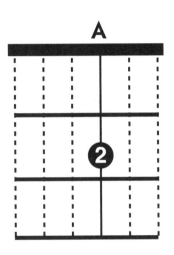

On the diagram to the right, indicate the fingering for the note A by placing the number "2" in a circle on the 2nd fret of the 3rd string.

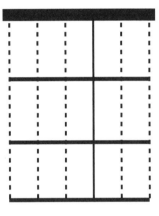

ACTIVITY: The Whole Note

A *whole note* lasts four beats.

How to Draw the Whole Note

Draw an oval in a space or on a line.

Now, draw four whole notes on spaces and four whole notes on lines.

Aura Lee

CD 1
Track 69

Elvis Presley recorded this folk song as a pop ballad called "Love Me Tender."

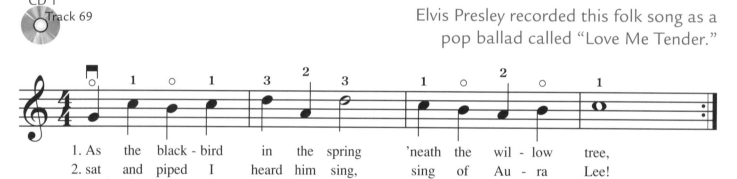

1. As the black - bird in the spring 'neath the wil - low tree,
2. sat and piped I heard him sing, sing of Au - ra Lee!

Au - ra Lee! Au - ra Lee! Maid of gold - en hair,

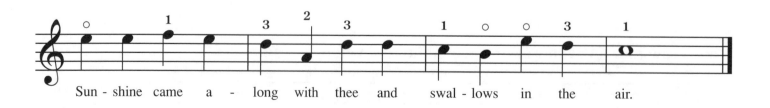

Sun - shine came a - long with thee and swal - lows in the air.

She'll Be Comin' 'Round the Mountain

CD 1
Track 70

G⁷   C

Hold down
1st finger

She'll be com - in' 'round the moun - tain when she comes.   She'll be

G⁷

com - in' 'round the moun - tain when she comes.   She'll be

com - in' 'round the moun - tain, she'll be com - in' 'round the moun - tain, she'll be

C

Hold down
1st finger

com - in' 'round the moun - tain when she comes!

Review: Music Matching Games

<table>
<tr><td>**Chords**</td><td>Draw a line to match each chord frame on the left to the correct photo on the right.</td></tr>
</table>

1.

2.

3.

4.

<table>
<tr><td>**Symbols**</td><td>Draw a line to match each symbol on the left to its name on the right.</td></tr>
</table>

1. o   **Treble clef**

2.   **Quarter note**

3.   **Whole note**

4.   **Quarter slash**

5.   **Half note**

6.   **Double bar line**

7.   **Half rest**

8.   **Repeat sign**

9.   **Quarter rest**

<table>
<tr><td>**Notes**</td><td>Draw a line to match each note on the left to its correct music notation on the right.</td></tr>
</table>

1.   

2.   

3.   

4.   

5.   

6.   

7.   

8.   

Answer Key

Chords
1: page 16; 2: page 20; 3: page 25; 4: page 31

Symbols
1: page 70; 2: page 63; 3: page 39; 4: page 10;
5: page 39; 6: page 28; 7: page 57; 8: page 18;
9: page 10

Notes
1: page 41; 2: page 46; 3: page 47; 4: page 52;
5: page 55; 6: page 59; 7: page 67; 8: page 70

Notes on the Fourth String
Introducing D

A note on the space below the staff is called D. You already know D on the 2nd string. This D is on the 4th string and sounds lower than D on the 2nd string. To play this note, pick the open 4th string.

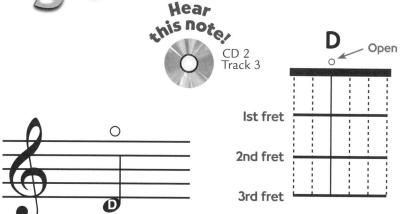

Hear this note!
CD 2
Track 3

CD 2
Track 4

D Warm-up

Four Open Strings

CD 2
Track 5

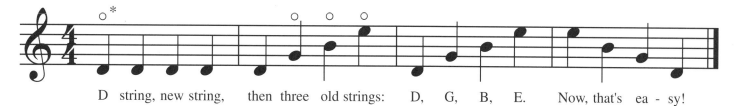

D string, new string, then three old strings: D, G, B, E. Now, that's ea-sy!

I Choose Guitar

CD 2
Track 6

Trum-pets, cel-los and the flute are ve-ry nice to lis-ten to,

but the in-stru-ment I choose to play is the gui-tar.

*A finger number is now only shown the first time a note appears in a tune.

75

ACTIVITY:
The Note D (4th String)

The note on the space below the staff is called D.

Drawing the Note D

To draw the note D on the staff, place the note-head on the space below the staff, and draw the stem up to the fourth line. On the staff below, draw the note D six times as quarter notes.

Playing the Note D

To play the note D,
pick the open 4th string.

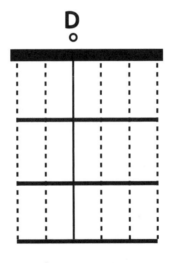

On the diagram to the right, indicate the fingering for the note D by placing "**o**" above the 4th string.

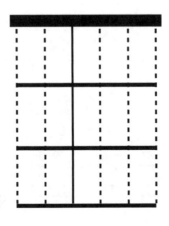

Introducing the Half-Note Slash

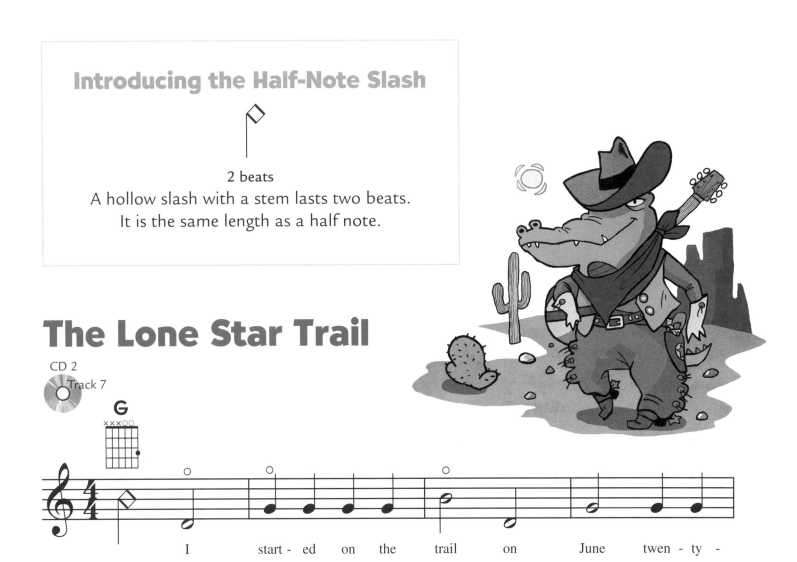

2 beats
A hollow slash with a stem lasts two beats.
It is the same length as a half note.

The Lone Star Trail

CD 2
Track 7

G

I start-ed on the trail on June twen-ty-

third. I been punch-in' Tex-as cat-tle on the Lone Star

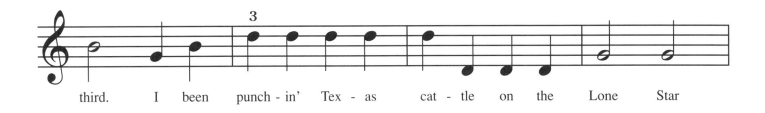

Trail, sing-in', "Ki - yi yip-pi yap-pi yay, yap-pi

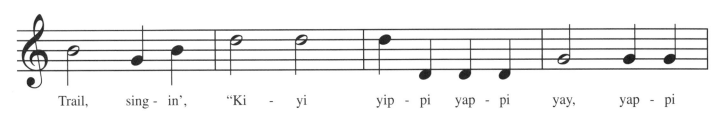

yay!" Sing-in', "Ki - yi yip-pi yap-pi yay!"—

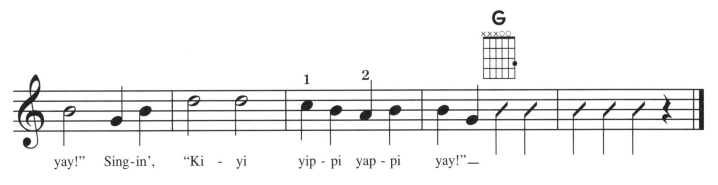

ACTIVITY: The Half-Note Slash

The *half-note slash* has a diamond-shaped notehead and a stem. Each half-note slash lasts two beats, which is the same length as a half note.

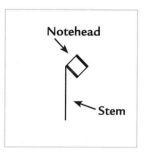

Notehead

Stem

How to Draw the Half-Note Slash

Step 1: Create the bottom half of the diamond-shaped notehead by drawing a "v" from the middle line to the second line.

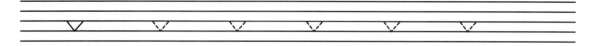

Step 2: Create the top half of the notehead by drawing an upside-down "v" from the middle line to the fourth line.

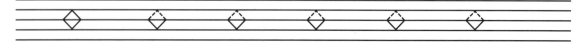

Step 3: Create the stem by drawing a line down from the left of the notehead to just below the staff.

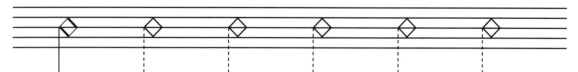

Now, draw six half-note slashes.

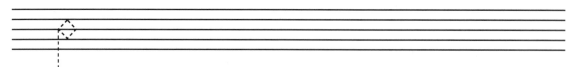

Counting Time

Fill in the missing beats with half-note slashes, and then write the counts below the staff.

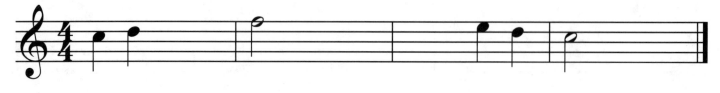

Introducing Four-String Chords

Now that you have learned the note D on the D string, you can add it to chords you already know to make four-string versions of those chords.

Hear this chord! CD 2 Track 8

The Four-String G Chord

This is the same as the three-string G chord, but you also strum the open D string.

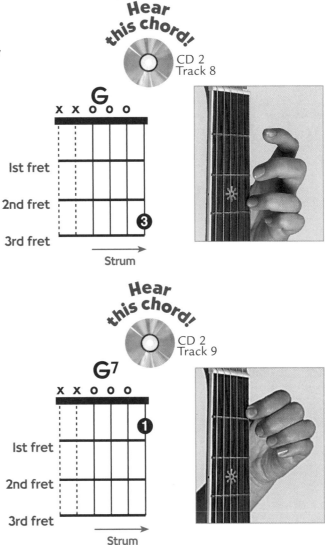

G
x x o o o o
1st fret
2nd fret
3rd fret
③
Strum

Hear this chord! CD 2 Track 9

The Four-String G⁷ Chord

This is the same as the three-string G^7 chord, but you also strum the open D string.

G⁷
x x o o o o
1st fret
①
2nd fret
3rd fret
Strum

New Chord Exercise

For this exercise, use the four-note G and G^7 chords, and also use the three-string C chord. A chord frame will be shown only the first time a chord is used. Play the chord the same way any time you see its symbol in the music again.

CD 2 Track 10

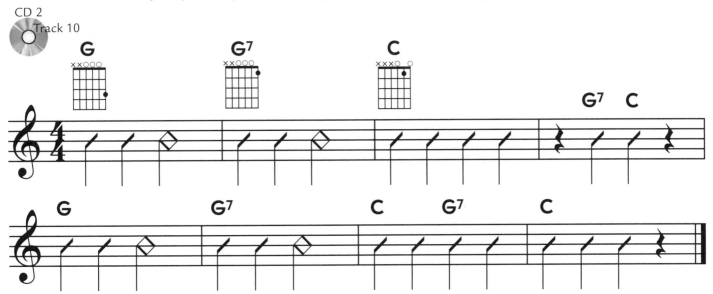

79

ACTIVITY: The Four-String G and G⁷ Chords

The Four-String G Chord

G
x x o o o

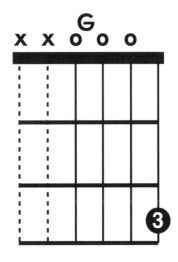

❸

Draw the missing **x**'s and **o**'s for this four-string G chord.

G

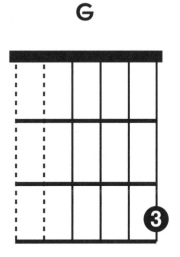

❸

The Four-String G⁷ Chord

G⁷
x x o o o

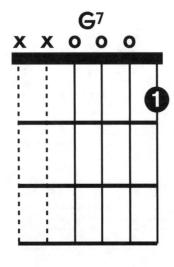

❶

Draw the missing **x**'s and **o**'s for this four-string G⁷ chord.

G⁷

❶

Rock Me Mozart

C

1

3

Mo - zart wrote some ve - ry cool mu - sic.

1   3

It   is   great   if   it's   slow   or   it's   quick.

G⁷

Rock - ing   to Wolf - gang Mo -   zart.

G   G⁷

All   the   mu - sic he   wrote was   art!

G   G⁷

Rock   me Mo - zart with your   real - ly rock - in'   tunes.   Yeah!

C

81

Notes on the Fourth String
Introducing E

A note on the lowest line of the staff is called E. You already know E that is the open 1st string. This E is on the 4th string and sounds lower. To play this note, use finger 2 to press the 4th string at the 2nd fret. Pick only the 4th string.

Hear this note!
CD 2
Track 12

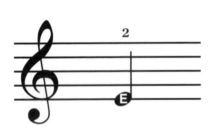

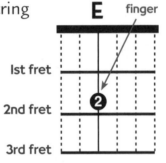

Second finger

E

1st fret

2nd fret

3rd fret

CD 2
Track 13

E Warm-up

CD 2
Track 14

On My Horse

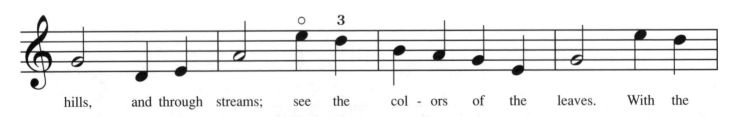

Rid - ing fast   on my horse;   gal - lop through the   trees,   ov - er

hills,   and through streams; see   the   col - ors of the   leaves. With the

wind   in my   hair,   I will   ride my love - ly   horse.

82

ACTIVITY: The Note E (4th String)

The note on the bottom line of the staff is called E.

Drawing the Note E

To draw the note E on the staff, place the notehead on the bottom line, and draw the stem up to just above the fourth line. On the staff below, draw the note E six times.

E

Playing the Note E

To play the note E, press the 4th string at the 2nd fret.

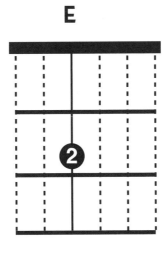

On the diagram to the right, indicate the fingering for the note E by placing the number "2" in a circle on the 2nd fret of the 4th string.

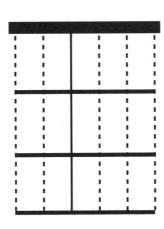

Old MacDonald Had a Farm

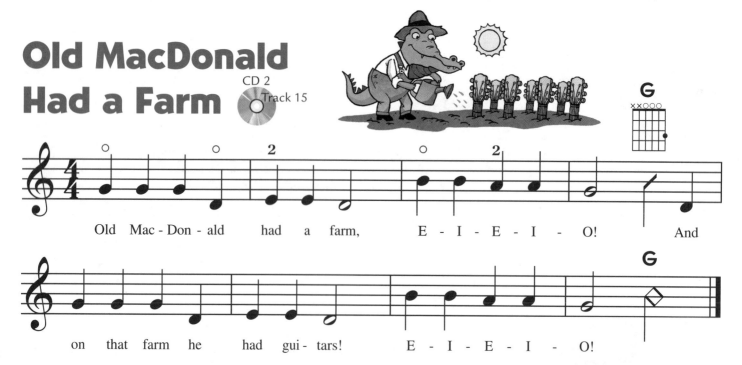

CD 2 Track 15

G

Old Mac-Don-ald   had   a   farm,   E - I - E - I - O!   And

on that farm he   had   gui-tars!   E - I - E - I - O!

G

The Four-String C Chord

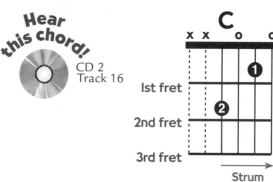

Hear this chord! CD 2 Track 16

C

This chord is the same as the three-string C chord, but you also put finger 2 on the 2nd fret of the 4th string.

1st fret
2nd fret
3rd fret
Strum

Introducing Common Time $\mathbf{C}$

This symbol is a time signature that means the same as $\frac{4}{4}$.

$\mathbf{C} = \frac{4}{4}$ The 4 on the top means there are 4 beats in each measure.
The 4 on the bottom means a quarter note gets 1 beat.

C Blues

CD 2 Track 17

Use the four-string C chord.

C

C

C

ACTIVITY:
The Four-String C Chord

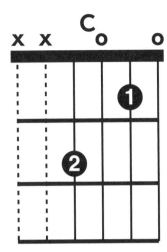

Draw the missing **x**'s and **o**'s for this four-string C chord.

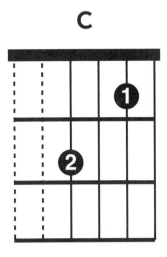

ACTIVITY:
Common Time

This symbol **𝄴** is a time signature that means the same as $\frac{4}{4}$ time. There are four beats to each measure.

How to Draw the Common Time Signature

Draw a letter "C" from the fourth line to the second line.

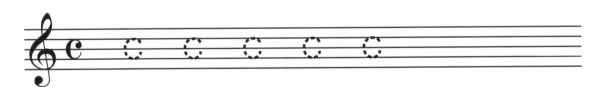

Now, draw six common time signatures.

ACTIVITY: Write Your Own Song with Four-String Chords

Here is your chance to write a song with four-string chords. Follow these steps.

1. Draw a treble clef at the beginning of each staff.

2. Draw a $\frac{4}{4}$ time signature next to the treble clef in the first measure.

3. Fill in the bar lines and draw a repeat sign at the end.

4. Draw quarter-note slashes, half-note slashes, quarter rests, and half rests. You can choose which beats have slashes and which have rests, but be sure there are exactly four beats in each measure.

5. Choose the four-string chords you want to use (G, G⁷, or C) by filling in the chord frame above each measure.

6. Make up your own lyrics and write them below each staff.

7. **Have fun** and play your song on your guitar.

Notes on the Fourth String
Introducing F

A note on the lowest space of the staff is called F. You already know F on the 1st string. This F is on the 4th string and sounds lower than F on the 1st string. To play this note, use finger 3 to press the 4th string at the 3rd fret. Pick only the 4th string.

Hear this note!

CD 2
Track 18

F

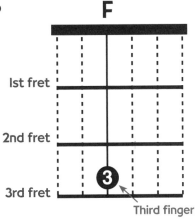

1st fret

2nd fret

3rd fret

Third finger

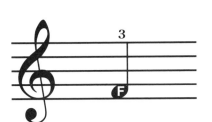

CD 2
Track 19

F Warm-up

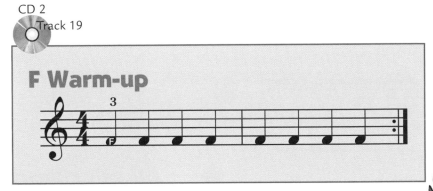

Baseball

Remember to use the four-string G⁷ chord.

CD 2
Track 20

G⁷

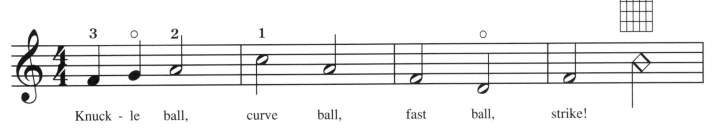

Knuck - le ball,   curve   ball,   fast   ball,   strike!

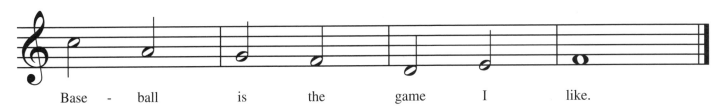

Base - ball   is   the   game   I   like.

ACTIVITY:
The Note F (4th String)

The note on the bottom space of the staff is called F.

Drawing the Note F

To draw the note F on the staff, place the notehead in the bottom space, and draw the stem up to the top line. On the staff below, draw the note F six times.

F

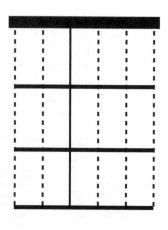

Playing the Note F

To play the note F, press the 4th string at the 3rd fret.

On the diagram to the right, indicate the fingering for the note F by placing the number "3" in a circle on the 3rd fret of the 4th string.

ACTIVITY: Notes on the Strings: D, E, F, G, and A

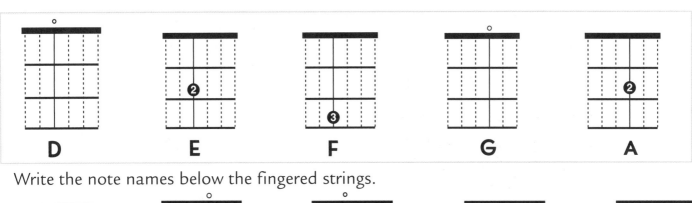

Write the note names below the fingered strings.

____   ____   ____   ____   ____

Draw each note on the staff above the note name. Use whole notes.

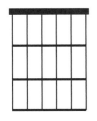
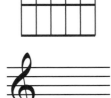

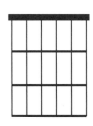

E   **G**   **D**   **F**   **A**

Draw the fingering on the fretboard diagram above each note.

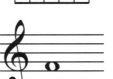

Write Your Own Melody with the Notes D, E, F, G, and A

Compose a short melody with the notes D, E, F, G, and A. Use quarter notes, half notes, and whole notes. Remember that only four beats fit in each measure.

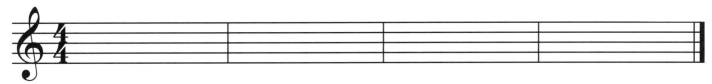

Reuben, Reuben

Remember to use the four-string C chord.

CD 2
Track 21

C

Reu - ben, Reu - ben, I've been think - ing what a weird world this would be

if the mon - keys lived in hous - es and we swung from tree to tree.

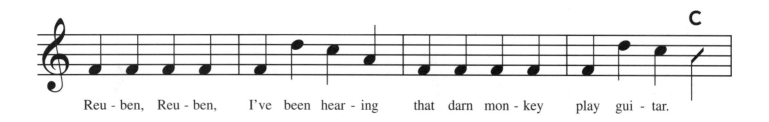

Reu - ben, Reu - ben, I've been hear - ing that darn mon - key play gui - tar.

He's been learn - ing ve - ry fast and knows the notes I've learned so far.

Dotted Half Notes & 3/4 Time

Introducing the Dotted Half Note

3 beats

This note looks like a half note, but with a dot to the right of the notehead. It lasts three beats.

The 3/4 Time Signature

A 3/4 time signature ("three-four time") means there are 3 equal beats in every measure.

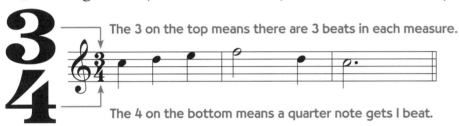

The 3 on the top means there are 3 beats in each measure.

The 4 on the bottom means a quarter note gets I beat.

CD 2
Track 22

Clap and Count out Loud

Count: 1 2 3   1 2 3   1 2 3   1 2 3

Three Is for Me!

CD 2
Track 23

One, two, three. One, two, three. Three is for me!

Play - ing in three with the great - est of ease.

ACTIVITY: The Dotted Half Note

The *dotted half note* lasts three beats.

How to Draw the Dotted Half Note

Step 1: Draw a half note.

Step 2: Add a dot to the right of the notehead.

Now, draw three dotted half notes with stems going up and three dotted half notes with stems going down.

ACTIVITY: The ¾ Time Signature

A ¾ time signature means there are three equal beats in every measure.

How to Draw the ¾ Time Signature

Step 1: Draw a number "3" sitting on top of the third line of the staff.

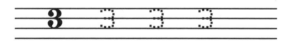

Step 2: Draw a number "4" sitting on the bottom line below the number 3.

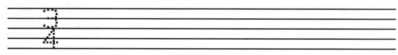

Now, draw six ¾ time signatures.

Choose the Time Signature

Each of the following examples has either three or four beats in each measure. Place either ⁴⁄₄, 𝄴, or ¾ at the beginning of each example. Use each time signature only once.

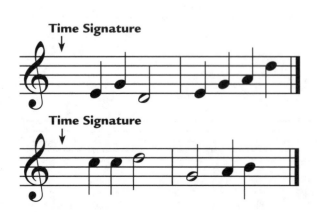

Daisy Bell

CD 2 Track 24

Playing Two Notes at Once

Sometimes, two notes are played at one time. In "Daisy Bell," usually when this happens one of the notes is an open string, but there are three places where both notes are fingered.

Dai - sy, Dai - sy, give me your

an - swer, do. I'm half

cra - zy all for the love of you. It

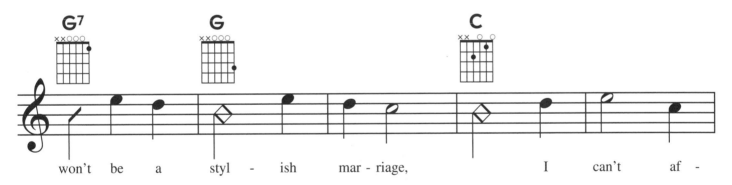

won't be a styl - ish mar - riage, I can't af -

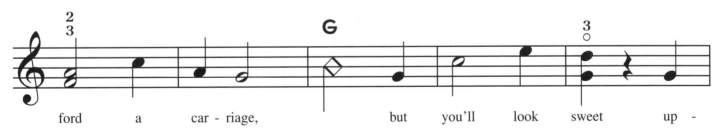

ford a car - riage, but you'll look sweet up -

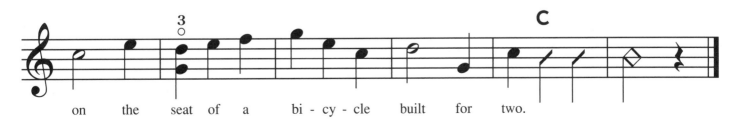

on the seat of a bi - cy - cle built for two.

Notes on the Fifth String
Introducing A

A line that extends the staff either up or down is called a *ledger line*. A note two ledger lines below the staff is called A. You already know A on the 3rd string. This A is the open 5th string and sounds lower than A on the 3rd string. To play this note, pick the open 5th string.

Hear this note!
CD 2
Track 25

← Ledger
← lines

A — Open
1st fret
2nd fret
3rd fret

CD 2
Track 26

A Warm-up

Five Open Strings

CD 2
Track 27

A D G B E, the op-en strings I'm play-ing.

Trash Truck

CD 2
Track 28

Trash truck, trash truck, makes the gar-bage go.

Trash truck, trash truck, the driv-er's name is Joe.

ACTIVITY:
The Note A (5th String)

The note A uses *ledger lines*. Ledger lines extend the staff up or down.

Drawing the Note A

Step 1:
Draw two short ledger lines below the staff.

Step 2:
Draw a notehead on the lowest ledger line.

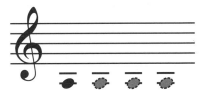

Step 3:
Add a stem going up from the right of the notehead.

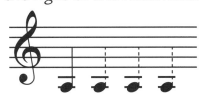

Playing the Note A

To play the note A, pick the open 5th string.

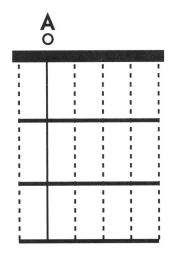

On the diagram to the right, indicate the fingering for the note A by placing "**o**" above the 5th string.

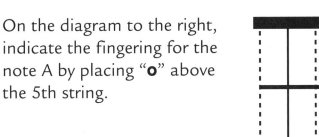

Scarborough Fair

Notes on the Fifth String
Introducing B

A note on the space one ledger line below the staff is called B. You already know B that is the open 2nd string. This B is on the 5th string and sounds lower than B on the 2nd string. To play this note, use finger 2 to press the 5th string at the 2nd fret. Pick only the 5th string.

Hear this note!
CD 2
Track 30

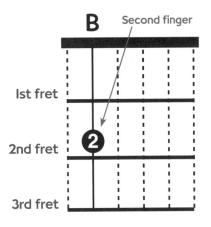

B   Second finger
1st fret
2nd fret   ②
3rd fret

CD 2
Track 31

B Warm-up

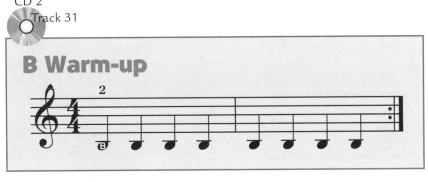

Cleaning Up
CD 2
Track 32

Clean - ing up my room is a spe - cial chore.

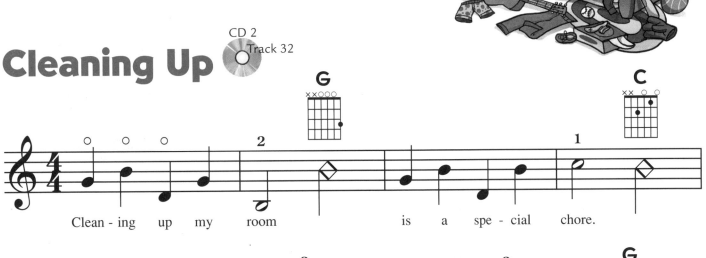

If I don't get done, I can't op - en my door!

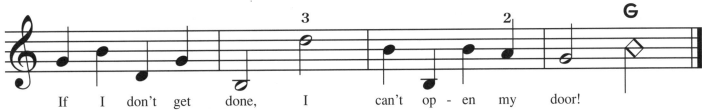

ACTIVITY: The Note B (5th String)

B is the same as A, but B is written on the space below just one ledger line.

Drawing the Note B

Step 1:
Draw one short ledger line below the staff.

Step 2:
Draw a notehead just below the ledger line.

Step 3:
Add a stem going up from the right of the notehead.

Playing the Note B

To play the note B, press the 5th string at the 2nd fret.

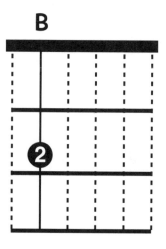

On the diagram to the right, indicate the fingering for the note B by placing the number "2" in a circle on the 2nd fret of the 5th string.

My Pet Cat

CD 2
Track 33

Run-ning af-ter my pet cat and my pet cat will chase a rat. And

once that rat runs in its hole, I'll catch my cat and that's my goal.

"Meow meow meow meow, meow meow meow meow, meow meow meow meow, meow meow." Crash!

Notes on the Fifth String
Introducing C

A note one ledger line below the staff is called C. You already know C on the 2nd string. This C is on the 5th string and sounds lower than C on the 2nd string. To play this note, use finger 3 to press the 5th string at the 3rd fret. Pick only the 5th string.

Hear this note!

CD 2
Track 34

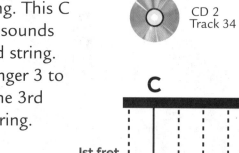

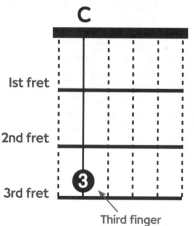

C

1st fret

2nd fret

3rd fret

3

Third finger

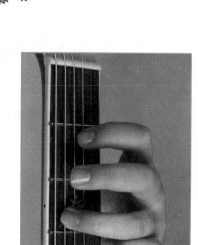

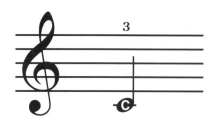

CD 2
Track 35

C Warm-up

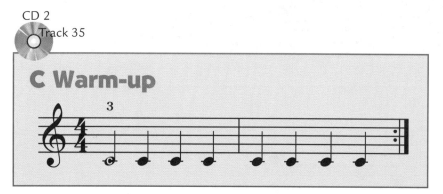

Barking Song

CD 2
Track 36

G

"Woof, woof, woof!   Woof, woof, woof!"   says Bel - la,   my   dog.

C

She will bark both   day and night, and   e - ven in the   fog.

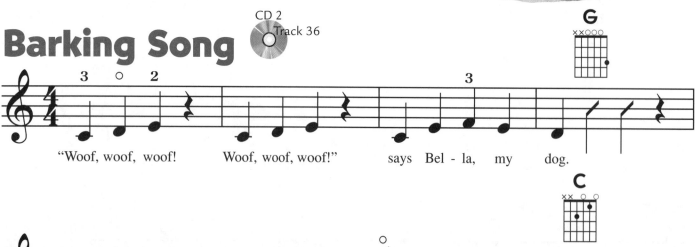

100

ACTIVITY: The Note C (5th String)

Drawing the Note C

Step 1:
Draw one short ledger line below the staff.

Step 2:
Draw a notehead on the ledger line.

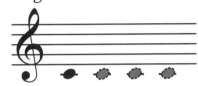

Step 3:
Add a stem going up from the right of the notehead.

Playing the Note C

To play the note C, press the 5th string at the 3rd fret.

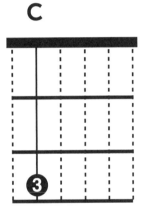

On the diagram to the right, indicate the fingering for the note C by placing the number "3" in a circle on the 3rd fret of the 5th string.

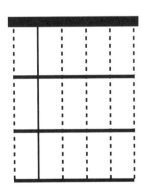

Draw the note C three times as quarter notes, then as half notes, and then as whole notes.

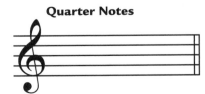

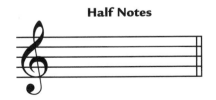

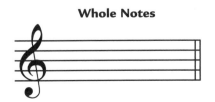

Volga Boatmen

CD 2
Track 37

Peter Gray

CD 2
Track 38

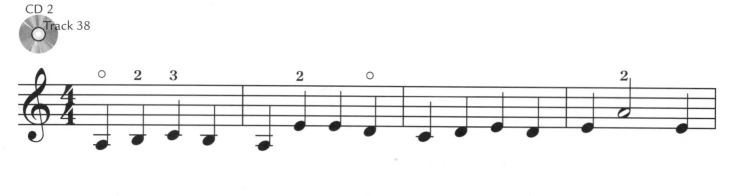

Liebesträum

This song was written in 1845 by
the famous composer Franz Liszt.
The title means "love dream."

CD 2
 Track 39

Introducing the Dotted-Half-Note Slash

The dotted-half-note slash is the
same length as a dotted half note.

3 beats

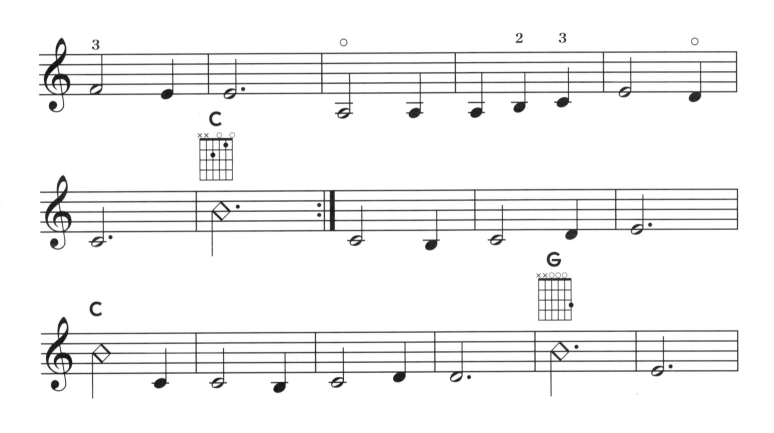

ACTIVITY: The Dotted-Half-Note Slash

The *dotted-half-note slash* lasts three beats, the same length as the dotted half note.

How to Draw the Dotted-Half-Note Slash

Step 1: Draw a half-note slash.

Step 2: Add a dot to the right of the notehead.

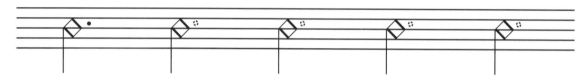

Now, draw six dotted-half-note slashes.

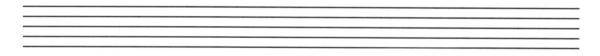

Write the Number of Beats

Here are all the types of notes, slashes, and rests you know so far. Write the number of beats each symbol receives (1, 2, 3, or 4) on the line below the staff.

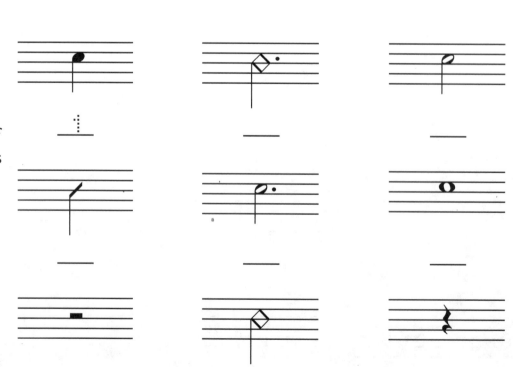

104

A Minor Boogie

CD 2
Track 40

105

Notes on the Sixth String
Introducing E

Hear this note! CD 2 Track 41

E — Open

A note on the space under the third ledger line below the staff is called E. This E is on the 6th string, and it is the lowest-sounding note on the guitar. To play this note, pick the open 6th string.

1st fret

2nd fret

3rd fret

CD 2 Track 42

E Warm-up

Six Open Strings

CD 2 Track 43

Now we have learned six op - en strings.

From high to low: E B G D A E.

Giraffe Under the Staff

CD 2 Track 44

Three lines be - low the staff hides a big,

tall gir - affe! Be care - ful if you

C

find him, be - cause you just might laugh!

C

106

ACTIVITY: The Note E (6th String)

Drawing the Note E

The note E uses ledger lines. Draw the ledger lines first, then the noteheads, and finish up by drawing the stems going up.

Now, draw E on the staff once as quarter notes, once as half notes, and once as whole notes.

Quarter Notes

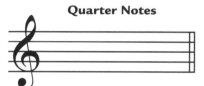

Half Notes

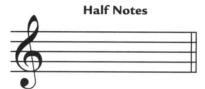

Whole Notes

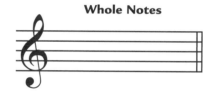

Playing the Note E

To play the note E, pick the open 6th string.

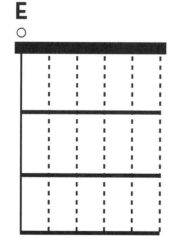

On the diagram to the right indicate the fingering for the note E by placing "**o**" above the 6th string.

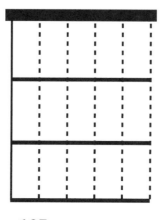

Two E's

C

There are two op-en E's on my gui-

G

tar: high E and low E. If

I use them right, I will go far. **C**

C

First-string E and sixth-string E will make me a big star!

Notes on the Sixth String
Introducing F

Hear this note!
CD 2
Track 46

A note on the third ledger line below the staff is called F. To play this note, use finger 1 to press the 6th string at the 1st fret. Pick only the 6th string.

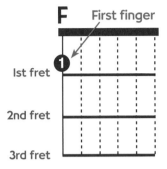

F
First finger
1st fret
2nd fret
3rd fret

CD 2
Track 47

F Warm-up

Dad's Classic Car

Introducing the Fermata

This symbol is a *fermata*. It is sometimes called a "bird's eye" because it looks like the eye of a bird. When you see a fermata over or under a note, play the note a little longer than it would normally be played. You should hold it about twice as long as usual.

CD 2
Track 48

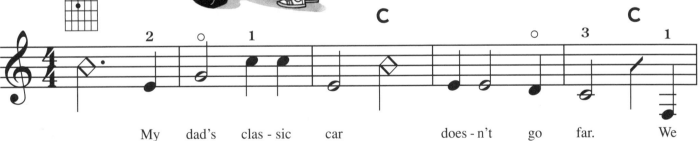

My dad's clas-sic car does-n't go far. We

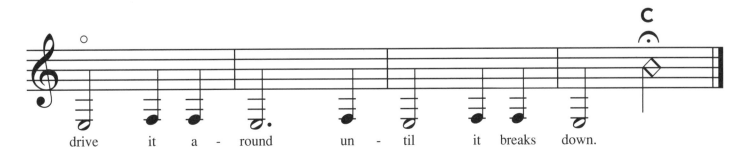

drive it a - round un - til it breaks down.

109

ACTIVITY: The Note F (6th String)

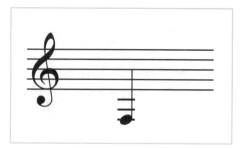

Drawing the Note F

The note F uses ledger lines. Draw the ledger lines first, then the noteheads, and finish up by drawing the stems going up.

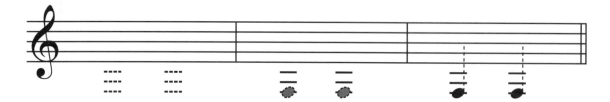

Now, draw F on the staff once as quarter notes, once as half notes, and once as whole notes.

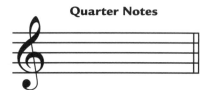

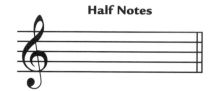

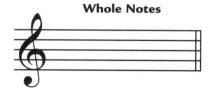

Playing the Note F

To play the note F, press the 6th string at the 1st fret.

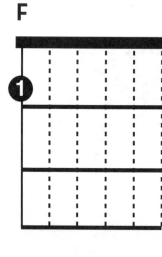

On the diagram to the right, indicate the fingering for the note F by placing the number "1" in a circle on the 1st fret of the 6th string.

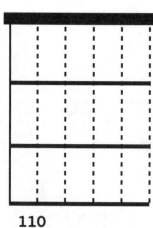

ACTIVITY: The Fermata

A *fermata* means to play the note a little longer than normal (usually about twice the normal length). The fermata is sometimes called a "bird's eye."

How to Draw the Fermata

Step 1: Draw the top half of a circle above the note.

Step 2: Place a dot inside the half circle.

Now, draw a fermata over each of the notes below.

Sakura

This song is one of Japan's most beautiful folk songs. The word *sakura* literally means "cherry blossom."

CD 2
Track 49

Sa - ku - ra,   Sa - ku - ra,   cher - ry   blos - soms

in   the   sky,   near   and   far   as   eye   can   see,

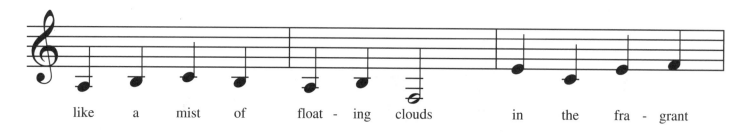

like   a   mist   of   float - ing   clouds   in   the   fra - grant

blush   of   spring.   Come,   oh   come.   Come,   oh   come.

Come   and   see   the   cher - ry   trees.

Notes on the Sixth String
Introducing G

A note on the space two ledger lines below the staff is called G. Use finger 3 to press the 6th string at the 3rd fret. Pick only the 6th string.

Hear this note!
CD 2
Track 50

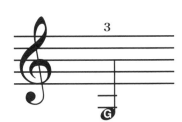

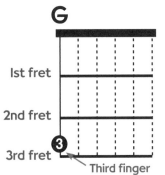

CD 2
Track 51

G Warm-up

All the Notes I Know So Far

CD 2
Track 52

From the low-est to the high-est, these are all the notes I know so far!

From the high-est to the low-est, play-ing all the notes is real-ly fun!

Do-Re-Mi Is for Me!

CD 2
Track 53

Using syllables like *Do* and *Re* for notes is called *solfège* ("sol-FEZH").

Do re mi fa sol la ti do. Do re mi fa sol.

Do ti la sol fa mi. Sol fa mi re do!

113

ACTIVITY:
The Note G (6th String)

The note on the space two ledger lines below the staff is called G.

Drawing the Note G

To draw the note G on the staff, first draw two ledger lines below the staff. Then, place the notehead in the space below the second ledger line and draw the stem up to the third line. On the staff to the right, draw the note G six times.

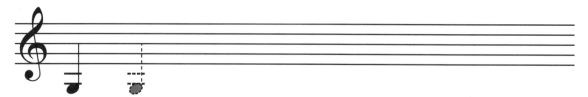

G

Playing the Note G

To play the note G, press the 6th string at the 3rd fret.

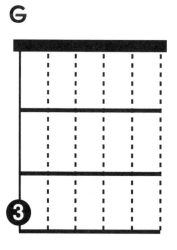

On the diagram to the right, indicate the fingering for the note G by placing the number "3" in a circle on the 3rd fret of the 6th string.

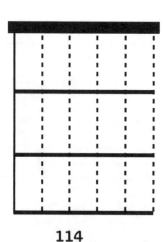

Spy Rock

I'm a spy for just the good guys, catch-ing bad guys right and left,

sec-ret gad-gets in my pock-ets, find-ing crooks be-fore a theft.

Bad guys run when they see me, I walk up and then they flee!

I'm a spy for you, now don't you want to be like me?

The Farmer in the Dell

CD 2
Track 55

The far - mer in the dell,

the far - mer in the dell.

Hi! Ho! The dai - ry -

o, the far - mer in the dell.

116

B.I.N.G.O.

CD 2
Track 56

C

There was a far - mer had a dog, and Bin - go was his

name - o. B - I - N - G - O, B - I -

N - G - O, B - I - N - G - O, and Bin - go was his name - o.

Introducing High A

Hear this note!

CD 2
Track 57

Just like ledger lines below the staff extend the staff lower, ledger lines above the staff extend the staff higher. The note one ledger line above the staff is called A. This A sounds higher than the other A's you've learned so far. To play high A, move your hand higher up the neck and use finger 4 to press the 1st string at the 5th fret.

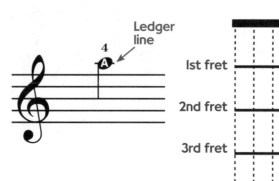

CD 2
Track 58

High A Warm-up

Back to Russia

CD 2
Track 59

Once up - on a time, long, long a - go, lived

Prin - cess An - a - sta - si - a in a place called Rus - sia.

She was chased a - way from there, ne - ver to re - turn back home.

Ma - ny hoped that she'd come back, she'd come back to Rus - sia.

ACTIVITY:
The Note High A (1st String)

The note one ledger line above the staff is called high A.

Drawing the Note High A

To draw the note high A on the staff, first draw one ledger line above the staff. Then, place the notehead on the ledger line and draw the stem down to the third line. On the staff to the right, draw the note high A six times.

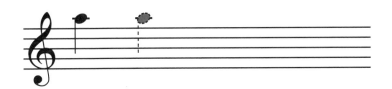

Playing the Note High A

To play the note high A, press the 1st string at the 5th fret.

On the diagram below, indicate the fingering for the note high A by placing the number "4" in a circle on the 5th fret of the 1st string.

A

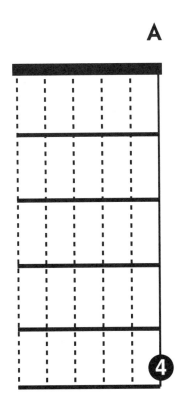

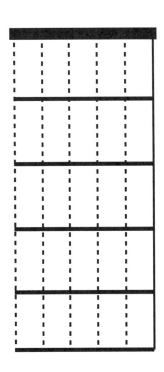

ACTIVITY:
Notes on the Strings:
E, F, G, A, B, C, and High A

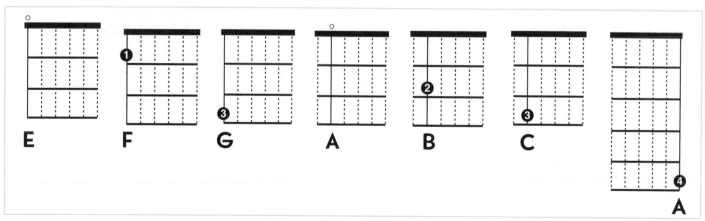

Write the correct note names below the fingered strings.

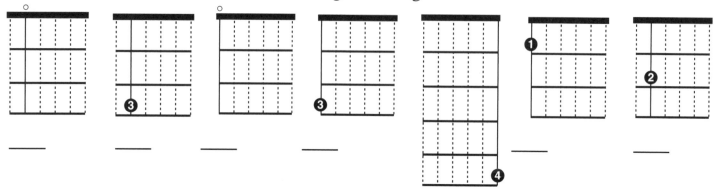

Draw the note on the staff above each note name. Use dotted half notes.

F   **A**   **C**   **High A**   **E**   **G**   **B**

Draw the fingering on the fretboard diagram above each note.

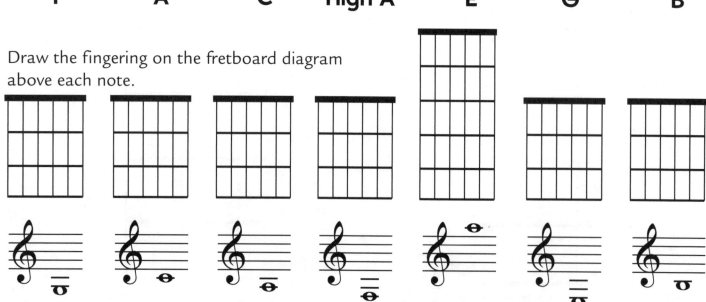

The Riddle Song

Gave my love a cher-ry that has no stone. I
gave my love a chick-en that has no bone. I
gave my love a ring—— that has no end. I
gave my love a ba-by that's not cry - in'.

121

Pickup Measures

Not all pieces of music begin on the first beat. Sometimes music begins with just part of a measure, which is called a *pickup*.

A pickup is like a pumpkin pie. If you were to cut the pie into four equal pieces and take one piece away, there would be three pieces left. If you are playing in 4/4 time and the pickup measure has one quarter note, there will be three quarter notes in the last measure.

Playing in 3/4 time is like cutting the pie into three equal pieces: if there is one quarter note as a pickup, there will be two quarter notes in the last measure.

CD 2
Track 61

Clap and Count out Loud

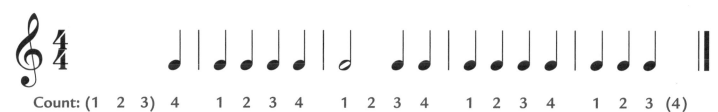

Count: (1 2 3) 4   1 2 3 4   1 2 3 4   1 2 3 4   1 2 3 (4)

A-Tisket, A-Tasket

CD 2
Track 62

C

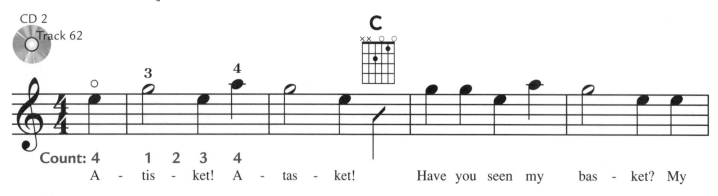

Count: 4   1 2 3 4
A - tis - ket! A - tas - ket!   Have you seen my bas - ket? My

moth - er sent me   to the mar - ket,   on the way I lost it.

1 2 3 4   1 2 3

122

ACTIVITY: Counting Time

For each example, write the counts for the pickup measure and the
final measure under the staff. Put parentheses around the counts
that aren't played.

(1) (2) (3) 4   1   2   3   (4)

___ ___ ___   ___ ___ ___

___ ___ ___   ___ ___ ___

___ ___ ___   ___ ___ ___

___ ___ ___   ___ ___ ___

The Yellow Rose of Texas

Tempo Signs

A *tempo sign* tells you how fast to play the music.
Below are the three most common tempo signs.

Andante ("ahn-DAHN-teh") **slow**

Moderato ("moh-deh-RAH-toh") **moderately**

Allegro ("ah-LAY-groh") **fast**

Three-Tempo Rock

Play three times: first time **Andante**, second time **Moderato**, third time **Allegro**.

Andante · CD 2 Track 64   Moderato · CD 2 Track 65   Allegro · CD 2 Track 66

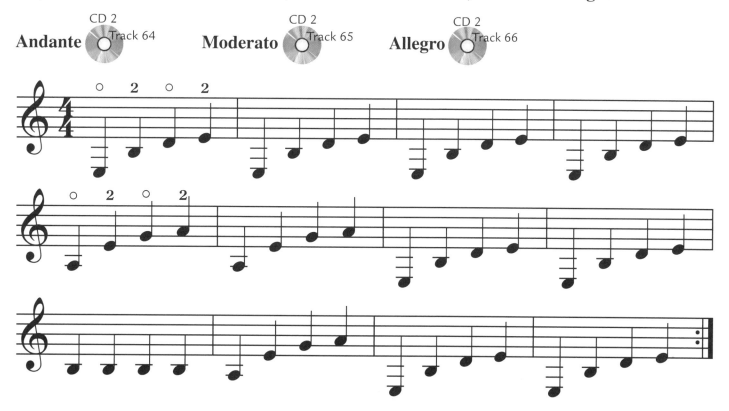

Writing Tempo Signs

Write the correct tempo sign next to the speed that matches.

slow _____   **moderately** _____   **fast** _____

125

1812 Overture

CD 2
Track 67

C

Allegro

Tchai - kov - sky's   o - ver - ture is   ex - plo - sive

with can - nons,   drums and horns and   tim - pa - ni.

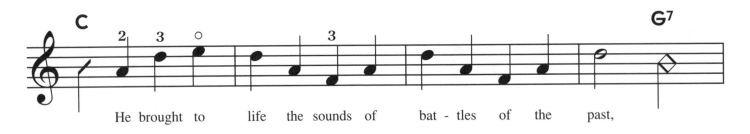

He brought to   life the sounds of   bat - tles of the   past,

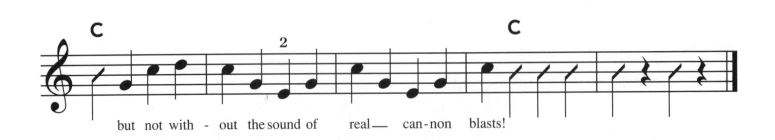

but not with - out the sound of   real — can - non blasts!

Reading Three-String Chords as Notes

Up until now, you have been reading chords as slash notes. When you are play a chord, you simply play three or more notes at the same time. Chords can also be shown as notes in the music. Here are some three-string chords you already know, shown as chords and as notes.

The Three-String C Chord

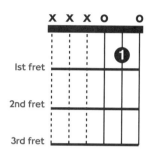 

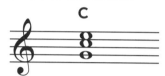
Here is the chord shown as notes.

The Three-String G Chord

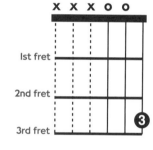 

Here is the chord shown as notes.

The Three-String G⁷ Chord

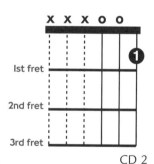 

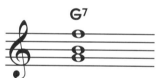
Here is the chord shown as notes.

Theme from Carmen

ACTIVITY: Three-String Chords as Notes

Three-String C Chord

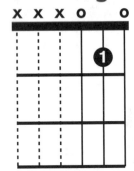

Here is the chord shown as notes.

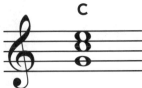

Write the three-string C chord as notes on the staff.

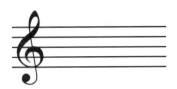

Three-String G Chord

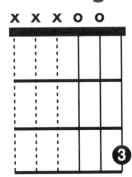

Here is the chord shown as notes.

Write the three-string G chord as notes on the staff.

Three-String G7 Chord

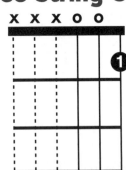

Here is the chord shown as notes.

Write the three-string G7 chord as notes on the staff.

Write three-note chords as notes on the staff below the chord names. Use quarter notes and half notes. Remember to use only four beats per measure because of the $\frac{4}{4}$ time signature.

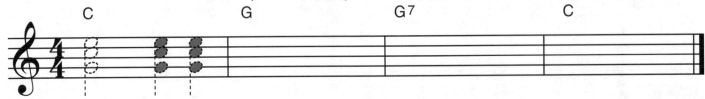

128

Reading Four-String Chords as Notes

Here are the four-string versions of the chords on the previous page, shown as chords and as notes.

CD 2
Track 72

The Four-String C Chord

CD 2
Track 73

The Four-String G Chord

CD 2
Track 74

The Four-String G⁷ Chord

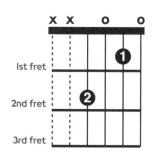

Here is the chord shown as notes.

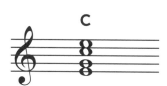

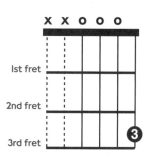

Here is the chord shown as notes.

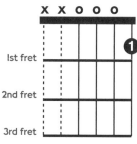

Here is the chord shown as notes.

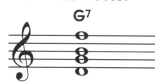

Rockin' with Chords

CD 2
Track 75

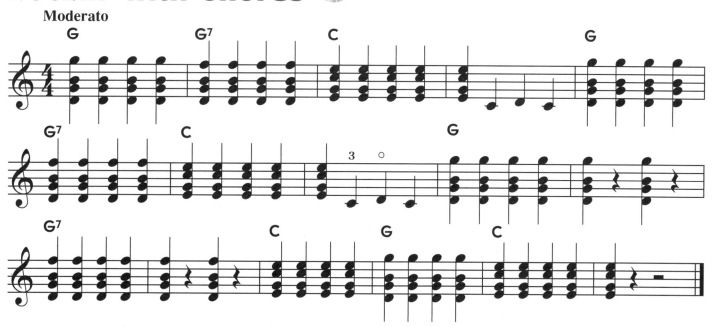

129

ACTIVITY: Four-String Chords as Notes

Four-String C Chord

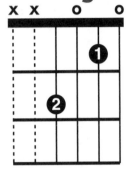

Here is the chord shown as notes.

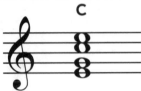

Write the four-string C chord as notes on the staff.

Four-String G Chord

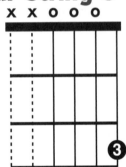

Here is the chord shown as notes.

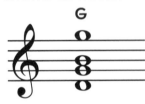

Write the four-string G chord as notes on the staff.

Four-String G⁷ Chord

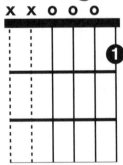

Here is the chord shown as notes.

Write the four-string G⁷ chord as notes on the staff.

Write four-note chords as notes on the staff below the chord names. Use quarter notes, half notes, and dotted half notes. Remember to use only three beats per measure because of the $\frac{3}{4}$ time signature.

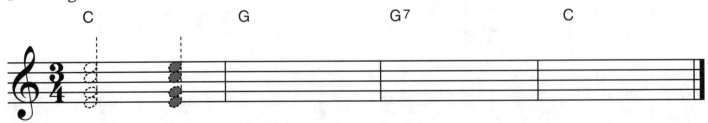

Bass-Chord Accompaniment

Now that you can read chords as notes, you can break them up by playing the lowest note of the chord, called the *bass note*, followed by the rest of the notes. We call this *bass-chord accompaniment*. There are two standard types of bass-chord accompaniments in $\frac{4}{4}$ time.

Bass-Chord-Chord-Chord

CD 2
Track 76

The first kind of bass-chord accompaniment is called *bass-chord-chord-chord* accompaniment. To play it, play the bass note once followed by the rest of the notes three times.

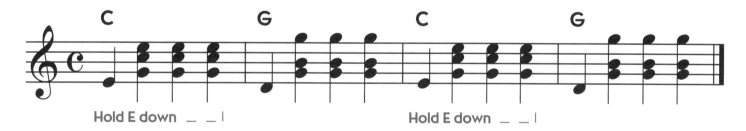

Hold E down _ _ | Hold E down _ _ |

Bass-Chord-Bass-Chord

CD 2
Track 77

The other type of bass-chord accompaniment in $\frac{4}{4}$ time is called *bass-chord-bass-chord* accompaniment. To play it, play the bass note once followed by the rest of the notes one time, and repeat the bass note followed by the rest of the notes again.

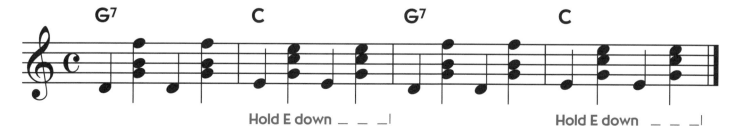

Hold E down _ _ _| Hold E down _ _ _|

131

Can-Can (duet)

CD 2 Track 78

"Can-Can" is a *duet*, which means there are two versions of music that are played at the same time. Part 1 is the *accompaniment* part. Play it slowly at first, and work out all the chords. Once you can play it without stopping, have your parent, teacher, or a friend play along with Part 2, the melody part, which is at the bottom of the page. You can also play along with the CD. Once you have played the duet a few times, switch parts and play the melody while someone else plays the accompaniment.

Part 1: Accompaniment CD 2 Track 79

Part 2: Melody CD 2 Track 80

Dynamics

Symbols that show how loud or soft to play are called *dynamics*. These symbols come from Italian words. Four of the most common dynamics are shown here.

p
piano
("PYAH-noh")
soft

mf
mezzo-forte
("MED-zoh FOHR-teh")
moderately loud

f
forte
("FOHR-teh")
loud

ff
fortissimo
("fohr-TEE-see-moh")
very loud

Theme from Beethoven's Fifth Symphony

CD 2
Track 81

Introducing the Whole Rest

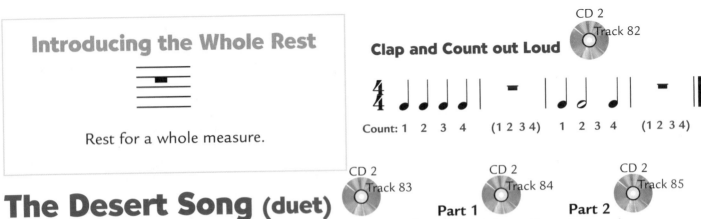

Rest for a whole measure.

Clap and Count out Loud
CD 2 Track 82

The Desert Song (duet)

CD 2 Track 83   Part 1 CD 2 Track 84   Part 2 CD 2 Track 85

Like "Can-Can" on page 132, "The Desert Song" is a duet. This time, Part 1 is written directly above Part 2. When you play Part 1 of the duet, only play the music on the staff labeled number 1. When you play Part 2, just play the music on the staff labeled number 2.

Echo Rock

CD 2 Track 86

134

ACTIVITY: Dynamics

Dynamics are symbols that tell you how loud or soft to play.
Below are the four most common dynamics.

p   stands for *piano*, which means **soft**.

mf   stands for *mezzo-forte*, which means **moderately loud**.

f   stands for *forte*, which means **loud**.

ff   stands for *fortissimo*, which means **very loud**.

Writing Dynamics

Write the correct dynamic sign next to its definition.

loud _____   very loud _____

soft _____   moderately loud _____

ACTIVITY: The Whole Rest

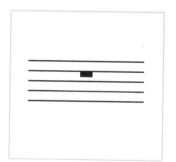

A *whole rest* means do not play for a whole measure.

How to Draw the Whole Rest

Step 1: Draw a box under the bottom of the middle line of the staff.

Step 2: Fill in the box.

Now, draw six whole rests.

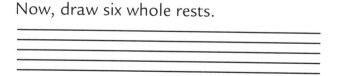

Notice that the whole rest and half rest look very similar. Remember that the half rest lasts a shorter time than the whole rest. You can think of it as the half rest being lighter, so it sits above the line, and the whole rest is heavier, so it falls below the line.

135

Ties

A *tie* is a curved line that connects two of the same note. When two notes are tied, don't play the second note, but keep the first note playing until the second note is done. You are really adding the two notes together.

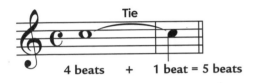

4 beats + 1 beat = 5 beats

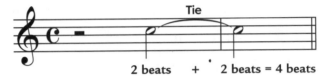

2 beats + 2 beats = 4 beats

Clap and Count out Loud

CD 2
Track 87

Count: 1 2 3 4 1 2 3 4 1 2 3 4 1 2 3 4

Shenandoah

CD 2
Track 88

Moderato
mf

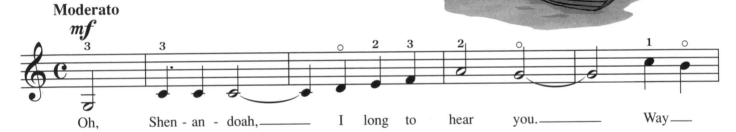

Oh, Shen - an - doah, I long to hear you. Way

hey, you rol - ling riv - er! Oh, Shen - an - doah,

I long to hear you. Way hey, we're bound a -

way a - cross the wide Mis - sou - ri.

136

ACTIVITY: Ties

A *tie* is a curved line that connects two of the same note. When two notes are tied, don't play the second note, but add the two notes together instead.

How to Draw the Tie

When the notes being tied are on or above the middle line of the staff, the curve of the tie goes up.

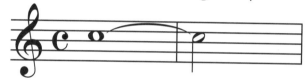

When the notes being tied are below the middle line of the staff, the curve of the tie goes down.

Draw ties to connect the notes below. Then write the total number of beats for each pair on the line below the staff.

5 beats

_____

_____

_____

_____

_____

When the Saints Go Marching In (duet)

CD 2
Track 89

Part 1 CD 2 Track 90

Part 2 CD 2 Track 91

Review: Music Matching Games

Chords

Draw a line to match each chord frame on the left to the correct notation on the right.

 1.

 2.

 3.

 4.

 5.

 6.

Notes

Draw a line to match each note on the left to its correct notation on the right.

1.

2.

3.

4.

5.

6.

7.

8.

9.

10.

Symbols

Draw a line to match each symbol on the left to its name or definition on the right.

1.   Dotted half note

2.   Whole rest

3. **3/4**   Half-note slash

4.   Dotted-half-note slash

5. ***ff***   Tie

6.   Three beats in a measure

7. **Moderato**   Fermata

8.   Common time

9. ***mf***   Loud

10. **C**   Moderately loud

11. **Allegro**   Soft

12. ***p***   Very loud

13. **Andante**   Slow

14.   Moderately

15. ***f***   Fast

Answer Key

Chords
1: page 127; 2: page 127; 3: page 127; 4: page 129
5: page 129; 6: page 129

Symbols
1: page 77; 2: page 136; 3: page 91; 4: page 91;
5: page 133; 6: page 134; 7: page 125; 8: page 103;
9: page 133; 10: page 84; 11: page 125; 12: page 133
13: page 125; 14: page 109; 15: page 133

Notes
1: page 106; 2: page 94; 3: page 75; 4: page 109;
5: page 113; 6: page 97; 7: page 100; 8: page 82
9: page 87; 10: page 118

Fingerboard Chart

STRINGS

6th 5th 4th 3rd 2nd 1st
E A D G B E

			STRINGS			
	6th	5th	4th	3rd	2nd	1st

FRETS

← Open →   E   A   D   G   B   E

← 1st Fret →   F   C   F

← 2nd Fret →   B   E   A

← 3rd Fret →   G   C   F   D   G

← 5th Fret →   A

Chord Encyclopedia

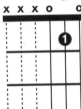

Here are all the chords you know.

The three-string C chord
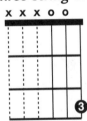

The three-string G chord
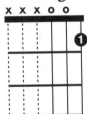

The three-string G⁷ chord

The three-string D⁷ chord

The four-string C chord
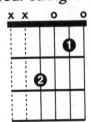

The four-string G chord
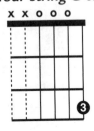

The four-string G⁷ chord
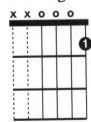